The Faith Unboxed

The Faith Unboxed

Andrew Petiprin

Published by Catholic Answers, Inc.
2020 Gillespie Way
El Cajon, California 92020
1-888-291-8000 orders
619-387-0042 fax
catholic.com

Printed in the United States of America

Cover design by ebooklaunch.com

Text layout by Nora Malone

978-1-68357-381-4
978-1-68357-382-1 Kindle
978-1-68357-383-8 ePub

In Memoriam

Eric K. Petiprin
For many years of loving conversations
about what things are and are not.

Contents

Acknowledgments

It was a great blessing and privilege to be introduced to the good people at Catholic Answers during a particularly uncertain time of my life. I am indebted to Todd Aglialoro for his interest in publishing this book, and to Drew Belsky for his careful, charitable editing of my work. Thanks are also due to Jon Sorensen for his generosity of spirit, and to Cy Kellett and the Catholic Answers Live team for opportunities to appear on air. Thanks also for the godly fellowship of Robert Mixa, Jared Zimmerer, Matt Nelson, and Joe Zambon. Finally, I am more grateful than ever to my family—my wife, Amber, and our two children, Alex and Aimee, whose love is the greatest earthly gift I could ever receive.

Introduction

When a person is contemplating whether to become or remain Catholic, he may struggle to understand or to agree with certain theological or moral doctrines. He may be concerned about aspects of the Church's liturgy or popular piety, or perhaps the clergy sex abuse scandals represent an enormous roadblock. Sometimes there are more personal and less rational hang-ups, like the prospect of being anonymous in an enormous parish. Or maybe it's fear of going to confession.

On my own faith journey, I have come to believe that every one of these matters related to whether one should join, remain in, or return to the Catholic faith ultimately comes down to one question: What *is* the Catholic faith?

This question is at the heart of the theological discipline called *ecclesiology*—a particularly tricky area in a world where we have less faith in organizations than we used to. Moreover, "inclusion" has become such a prized idea in our society that it would seem unjust if not simply absurd to many people to recognize any barriers to entry, let alone any standards required to maintain one's place within it. And sadly, the Catholic Church has leaned the way of most religious groups in recent decades, sometimes downplaying its members' inescapable obligations. To outsiders, but increasingly to insiders. too, the Catholic faith has become just one particularly large religious option to choose—or, more likely, *not* choose.

And yet, the Catholic Church's official claims about itself reject the notion that the Faith, or the Church, is just one option among many for the private expression of faith. The Faith is not my box in which I may put what I like. Nor is it a box containing just one thing that a religious consumer may take out, examine, and enjoy at the expense of shelves full of other things. And if it were possible to do an online "unboxing" of the Faith, the video would have certain things in common with conventional words often associated with it . . . but the unboxing would reveal much more.

The Faith is bigger than any institutional box. It is more than a denomination, a club, or an ideology. If a person is looking to escape the world by turning to the Catholic faith, he has chosen the wrong box. Likewise, the Faith is not a prison for self-loathers who are afraid of freedom. Nor again do the Faith's precepts underlie a dictatorship imposed upon people who would prefer to be free but are held down by the pope's oppressive red slipper. Finally, being Catholic is more than a feeling, and more than an individual preference for self-actualization.

When we unbox the Faith, we find it fits no categories and resists all labels.

In my journey into the Faith, I have found it helpful to approach the Faith from many angles as a way of articulating what it actually is. In an age where the Church is increasingly caricatured and regarded in a negative light (if it is regarded at all), a good way to talk about why someone would want to join it or stay in it may be to confront some of these misperceptions—to think outside the box.

Unboxed in the Bible

From the beginning of the Church, people have wondered what the Catholic faith is. A big part of St. Paul's work, as reflected in his letters to the early churches, is clarifying how the Church, and the Faith that it represents, is bigger than the first Christians' expectations and desires.

To the Galatians, Paul had to explain that belonging to the Church does not require first becoming Jewish. But he also needed to make it clear that there is nothing wrong with coming into Christianity from Judaism! To the Philippians, he explained that the Church is not a place of self-fulfillment, but rather where like-minded sacrifice is required. To the Ephesians, he taught that there is vast, desirable diversity among the unified believers, but that pagan morality is incompatible with the Church's life. To the Romans, he explained how the Church is in continuity with Israel, and how Jesus is the sinless recapitulation of sinful Adam.

Perhaps most interesting is Paul's need to clear up a number of misconceptions among the Corinthians, whose false impressions about what they belonged to may resonate with today's Christians better than any of the previous examples.

First, some of the Corinthians mistook their local assembly for a cult of personality centered on a man named Apollos. Paul corrected them: "I planted, Apollos watered, but God gave the growth" (1 Cor. 3:6). Second, some of the Corinthians believed that their membership in the Church granted them a freedom in Christ that permitted immorality. Responding to the rumor that there was a Corinthian Christian shacking up with his mother-in-law, Paul exclaimed, "You are arrogant! Ought you not rather to mourn? Let him who has done this be removed from among you" (5:2).

Finally, Paul corrected the Corinthians on their misunderstanding of individual status among members of the Church.

The Church was and remains today one body, with no spare parts. No spiritual gifts exceed any others in importance, and no social class has greater priority in gaining access to the sacraments. Paul explained to his ancient audience, and to us, too, that there was and is an animating principle for unity in the one, inseparable body of Christ, and that principle is the divine virtue of charity. The famous thirteenth chapter of 1 Corinthians begins, "If I speak in the tongues of men and of angels, but have not love, I am a noisy gong or a clanging cymbal."

Churchmen Apologize

In the era after Paul's death, new Christian apologists had to set the record straight about new misperceptions of what the Faith and the Church were and were not. That's the job of an *apologist*—not to beg for forgiveness, but to make the case for something.

In the second century, one such apologist, St. Justin Martyr, also known as Justin the Philosopher, was confronted with the charge that Christians were atheists—that is, because the Catholic Church did not worship the pagan gods of the Roman Empire, its members were thought to have *no* god. Justin replied, "We are godless with reference to beings like these who are commonly thought of as gods, but not with reference to the most true God."[1] Justin went even further, noting that the Catholic Church did hold that the pagan gods had power over men, but that Christians called such powers demons and avoided them.

In another example from the second and third centuries, the Catholic Church was accused of being a house of cannibalism. After all, Christians claimed to eat their God, Jesus Christ. In a dialogue called "Octavius," a Roman rhetorician and Christian apologist named Minucius Felix sought to address many false claims against the Church, including the charge of cannibalism, by use of reason. Octavius, a Christian, explains to his friend Caecilius, a pagan, that not only do Christians not eat human flesh, but "to us it is not lawful either to see or to hear of homicide."[2]

Examples abound through the centuries, reaching a crisis point among Christians in the Protestant Reformation. Among the many false claims Martin Luther and his successors made about the Catholic Church, perhaps the biggest one is the idea that there was once a true church, but that at some point in history, the Roman Catholic Church either had ceased to be it or had never really been it in the first place. Sadly, even some Catholics today assume that there was once a purer or better version of the Church than there is today.

But as St. John Henry Newman concluded after many years of considering the claims of his own Anglican tradition, the evidence in favor of the Catholic Church's continuity and flourishing in its God-given role in the world was much stronger than the evidence for its deterioration and abandonment of its identity. No matter how far back in Church history Newman went, he could never seem to find the *real* Church he was looking for. He described his findings in his masterful spiritual memoir, *Apologia Pro Vita Sua*:

> The drama of religion, and the combat of truth and error, were ever one and the same. The principles and proceedings of the Church now, were those of the Church then; the principles and proceedings of heretics then, were those of Protestants now.[3]

"What is the Catholic faith?" There are as many wrong answers as there are people to propose them. In this book, I propose to tackle eight of them from our own era—and thus to "apologize for" the Church, and the Faith, as we see them today.

Be a Child

My ultimate hope with this modest book is to encourage the reader to face the Catholic Church as it really is, and thereby foster a sense of belonging there. This is a book for people contemplating becoming Catholic, but it is equally suited for Catholics looking to feel more comfortable in their ecclesial home. It is a book for the merely curious, too, although nowhere do I conceal my hope that their open minds may soon close on the truth.

The essence of the Catholic faith is inherently countercultural. But "countercultural" need not mean antagonism to people who do not see the Church's point of view. Rather, in this book, I want to suggest that the Catholic faith can be and should be the underlying engine of identity in a shifting culture longing to stand on solid ground. The Catholic faith matters now, as ever, because it says that the mystery of God in Christ is more real than real, and that life in the Church is not just a pastime for a self-selected few either who do not have enough to do or whose "thing" is, inexplicably, religion.

An invitation to Christianity, and to the Catholic faith, assumes a vivid imagination that is too often ignored or misplaced in the cold, relativistic mainstream in which we swim. Like the parents at the end of the Christmas book and film *The Polar Express*, our grown-up culture has convinced itself that there is nothing beyond the materials that we can immediately see. Or if there is something more than meets the eye, it is subject to each person's experience and relegated to a publicly ignored "private" life. But children rightly reject this faux realism. They can also see through phony answers and are less prone to embarrassment in pointing out when something doesn't make sense. They hear the bell ringing, and we can open our ears to hear it, too.

Jesus affirms in several verses of Scripture the need for a childlike disposition. In one of the most famous ones, he declares, "Unless you turn and become like children, you will never enter the kingdom of heaven" (Matt. 18:3; see also Mark 10:13-16, Luke 18:15-17). I appeal to you, therefore, in the spirit of childlike trust, to see and to hear what the world tells you is foolish, dangerous, or simply impossible. I invite you in the pages of this book to explore the house of God, either for the first time or *as if* for the first time. I have not found the journey to the Catholic faith either boring or safe, as the great saints and teachers of the Faith demonstrate much more vividly. It is a love story, and love can hurt as much as it comforts. I admit, I have not always liked the answers the Church has given me when I have asked, at least not at first.

One of my previous books, *Truth Matters: Knowing God and Yourself*, is a precursor to this book in certain ways, although it is by no means necessary for you to have read it before you read this one. I wrote that book as a Protestant, but by the time I finished it, I knew I had no place to turn but into the arms of the Catholic Church. In that book, I followed the lead of C.S. Lewis, one of my greatest heroes in the Christian faith, in defending a doctrinal structure for Christianity that could be applied among different Christian groups. Lewis noted in the preface to his famous apologetical text *Mere Christianity* that his job was to bring seekers after truth into a hall, but that eventually a person must enter a room, where "there are fires and chairs and meals."[4] Lewis resolutely refused to say which room is the right one. But I found it.

In the sixth book of Lewis's *Chronicles of Narnia* series, *The Silver Chair*, there is a decisive moment for Jill Pole, one of the protagonists. She is dying of thirst and is compelled to drink . . . but as she approaches the stream, she is confronted by a ferocious lion, who the reader knows to be Aslan, the Christ figure. She tries to negotiate with him, to get a sense of whether she will be safe. He makes no promises, and in fact, he points out how truly dangerous he can be. Yet he also tells her repeatedly, "If you're thirsty, you may drink"[5]—and, moreover, "there is no other stream."

Lewis died an Anglican, not a Catholic, but many of his most devoted readers, including me, have concluded that "there is no other stream" from which to nourish ourselves than the Catholic faith. In this book, therefore, I invite you to drink. The Catholic Church stands before you in both its glory and its ignominy as the place for Christians to belong.

This book is not meant to be an indictment of non-Christians or of Christians outside the Catholic Church. It is not meant to belittle people who have the misperceptions about the Catholic Church that I seek to dispel. Rather, this book is meant as an encouragement to listen attentively to the God who answers our questions.

I pray that this little volume may be a means for God to answer some of yours.

CHAPTER I

The Ideology Box

I grew up in a relatively conservative home. My mother was a devout Protestant and raised us going to services and to Sunday school, singing in the choir, going to youth group, and most importantly reading Scripture and praying together at home. My father was a United States Navy officer and an extremely patriotic American, who had traveled the world, spoke fluent French, and loved the finer things from European culture.

I remember an early coming-of-age moment for me politically when I penned an impassioned but barely informed op-ed for my middle school newspaper in 1992, arguing why George H.W. Bush deserved a second term in the White House instead of Bill Clinton. I was shocked when our school's mock election returned the result of a Clinton victory, and when the same result ensued in real life, I remember my father muttering about an interloper, Ross Perot, who had wrecked everything for the Republican incumbent by entering the race as an independent candidate.

But the next day, things went back to normal. My dad was still pro-military, and my mom was still pro-life, but there was no large-scale critique of the culture or human solutions for a better world at our house. We went to church a lot, we took school seriously, we played sports, and from my perspective, we got along with everybody. We weren't perfect (more anon), but basic Christian teachings—albeit in a Protestant, not Catholic context—were our guiding lights. We were religious far more than political.

Politics, however, is unavoidable. A certain type of conservative person tends to regard politics as an always-imperfect attempt to organize and act on specific common human needs, preferably as locally and as minimally as possible. This was my parents' and much of my extended family's perspective. A certain type of progressive, on the other hand, views politics as more comprehensive, with all aspects of life subjected to the will of a national or international organization rooted in universally applied principles. When I was a kid, other members of my extended family tended to think this way, and I did, too, for a time in my teens and twenties. In any case, neither someone disposed more to conservative politics nor someone inclined to progressive politics need necessarily be ideological (though the latter most often does).

Where does the Catholic Church fit in all this? Is it conservative? Is it liberal? To find out, we will look inside these and other ideological boxes to get a sense of where (or whether) we find the Church of Jesus Christ.

Conservatism: The Non-Ideological Ideology

The word *ideology* is composed of two Greek words. The first is *idea*, meaning just about the same thing it means in English—a pattern of thought. The second is *logos*, a familiar suffix literally meaning "word," but more broadly denoting something written down for the purpose of study. Ideology, then, is the written expression of a system of ideas. It is the proposal of a theory, which is meant to solve problems when put into practice. It is an attempt to fit the truth into one convenient box.

In English, if a word ends in *-ism*, it is likely to be some form of ideology. As we open these boxes, let's start with an *-ism* that consciously tries to avoid inclusion as an ideology: conservatism.

Adherents to conservatism (i.e., conservatives) tend to advocate a theory, which, paradoxically, says that theories are a bad place to start from when thinking about people, systems, and societies. Conservatism also tends to focus on *not* doing something, or at least not doing something quickly, rather than running the risk of making the wrong choice. The debates among conservatives, then, revolve around what is worth conserving and what the principles are that guide decisions to keep things the same or make changes. The great American conservative thinker Russell Kirk, for example, noted that "any informed conservative is reluctant to condense profound and intricate intellectual systems to a few pretentious phrases," and "conservatism is not a fixed and immutable body of dogmata."[6]

Like Kirk, the well-known British conservative Roger Scruton often noted how a conservative tends to avoid ideology, since conservatism is more of a temperament than a strategy, often incorporating ideas from various ideologies, including liberalism. In fact, if conservatism may be considered an ideology, it is more a mournful reflection on the past rather than a prescription for the future.

In some key respects, conservatism is the natural bedfellow of a Catholic view of reality. Kirk, an adult convert to the Catholic Church, believed that conservatism first of all stands for "belief in a transcendent order, or body of natural law, which rules society as well as conscience." That is, God is in control. For example, ancient Israel preserved and revived its traditions over three centuries, rejoicing in the stability that an immutable law of God offered them. When Jesus came as the Messiah of Israel, he affirmed the traditions of his people as revealed by God. He said in the Sermon on the Mount, "Think not that I have come to abolish the law and the prophets; I have come not to abolish them but to fulfil them" (Matt. 5:17).

But in other ways, Christianity is not conservative at all—not entirely rooted, anyway, in the past or in the loss of what was once great. Jesus said and did radical things that upended his people's notions of what the Law and the Prophets were meant to conserve in the first place. He talked about his own body, for example, as the true temple instead of the magnificent structure in Jerusalem first built by King Solomon and then restored by Herod around the time of Christ. In one memorable scene where Jesus was in the Temple, he drove the moneychangers from the Court of the Gentiles and declared, "Destroy this temple, and in three days I will raise it up." This was not an idea most Jews would have expected or wanted to hear.

Liberalism: The Ideology of Ideologies

Liberalism works differently. Unlike conservatism, which resists being an ideology at all, liberalism is an umbrella under which many, if not all, modern ideologies may be gathered. It is *the* ideology.

Karl Marx was not the first liberal; in fact, he belongs on one end of a long spectrum of thinkers that includes not only Voltaire and Jean-Jacques Rousseau, but also David Hume and Adam Smith. Many classical liberals, including Smith, would now be considered by some conservative, but this whole lot, along with their many latter-day successors, have an important principle in common: the implicit or explicit rejection of Christianity as the basis of reality. Marx simply took to its logical end what is implied by earlier thinkers' exaltation of human reason above obedience to divine revelation. That is, something else—not the kingdom of heaven—is man's ultimate goal.

Marx diagnosed the malady afflicting the human condition not as the original sin of man's turning away from God, but rather an animalistic evolution of the struggle between an oppressive few and oppressed masses. Perfecting the science of economics would, in time, lead to man's salvation. In their famous *Communist Manifesto*, Marx and his partner, Friedrich Engels, began with a new spiritual declaration, superseding God and the gods of old: "A specter is haunting Europe—the specter of communism."[7] This is how ideology works, as an intangible substitute for revealed religion.

What vs. Why

Although there are few avowed communists in Western democracies nowadays, and almost none in the United States, both right and left tend to be more ideological, and therefore more liberal in one way or another, than they are Christian in the pre-modern sense. In practice, most people of all political groups are this-worldly, and functionally non-Christian. A pair of *-isms* older than Marxism explains why.

Highly relevant to modern people today is the one-two ideological combination of *rationalism* and *scientism*. For simplicity's sake, we can identify the seventeenth-century French philosopher René Descartes as the father of modern rationalism, which theorizes that reason, not experience, is the foundation of knowing anything to be true. But if we're skeptical about everything, depending on the priority of reason to arrive at truth, how do we know that we are real and capable of reasoning? Descartes's explanation is embedded in his famous phrase "cogito ergo sum," or "I think, therefore I am." A person of faith might justly wonder, isn't a rationalist still believing in something—namely, reason?

Nonetheless, around Descartes's time, it appeared that reason's moment of domination over superstition had arrived. Descartes was a little younger than Johannes Kepler and a near contemporary of Galileo Galilei. Isaac Newton was born seven years before Descartes died. It was a new world in which what had been relegated to the realm of mystery was suddenly explicable in the language of science. Science suddenly appeared to be a system that unlocked mysteries, presided over by a new quasi-religious class of elites. Scientists stood atop the pyramid of scientism as a new kind of shaman.

Innovations abounded in the next few centuries, with the Industrial Revolution transforming the world in the nineteenth and twentieth centuries and the digital revolution doing so again in our own age, even more drastically. Diseases have been cured. Toilets flush. Wars have been won. It is hard to argue with the results. Likewise, few are interested in considering any other explanations or solutions to the problems of the world than what fits into the scientific paradigm.

Luigi Giussani describes the rise to total dominance of scientism in the following way:

> It is a conception whereby scientific progress is promoted as the only true form of human enhancement, and used therefore, as the yardstick for all forms of development.[8]

Today, if science cannot explain something, it is as if it is not real. And what people choose to value as real, but what science ignores or dismisses, is subordinated to the private realm of opinion and preference—our own small boxes in which each of us first places and later finds his own meaning. But a crisis is now upon us as it becomes clearer that scientists may possess greater technical skill than ever, but at the same time, they lack the moral and philosophical formation to understand all the repercussions of their innovations.

As Ian Malcolm says in *Jurassic Park*, "Scientists were so preoccupied with whether or not they *could* that they didn't stop to think if they *should*." We may rejoice that new cancer treatments are available all the time, but do we stop to ask why there is so much more cancer now than there used to be? We may enjoy using our smart devices to get into ballgames without paper tickets, but shouldn't it bother us that they are constantly gathering information about us in order to sell us things? And what about the nearly 14,000 nuclear warheads in the world—just a few of which could destroy the entire planet—given to us by scientists working for governments?

And speaking of governments, there are all kinds of ideological sub-groups beneath liberalism, almost all of which take rationalism and scientism for granted as the way things are: authoritarianism, libertarianism, anarchism, nationalism, populism, socialism, communism, and fascism, to name just a few. In these more specific ideologies, a word stands for a collection of ideas that fit together to describe what one group or another considers the best way to manage government, the economy, and society as a whole within the liberal paradigm.

Definitions of different ideologies are usually imprecise, but they are meant to gather different assumptions about human nature and prescribe the means of achieving different ends like the common good, the greatest good, universal brotherhood, human freedom, national unity, and all sorts of other stated goals. For example, communism and fascism are both likely to be expressions of militaristic authoritarianism, but whereas communism is premised upon the State's ownership of everything, fascism usually allows private industry and profit, provided that companies serve the interest of the State.

Whoa . . . Wokeism

All of the *-isms* I've noted above fall into the realm of the political and are contentious. In a stable, civilized society, ideological factions are weak, and concepts from various ideologies may be debated, incorporated, or rejected without great turmoil. In a fractured, barbarous age, however, ideology is king, and it is often the basis for riots, terrorism, and even wars. Some adherents to various ideologies are proud to bear the name and use a specific set of jargon unique to their worldview, whereas others are tagged with unwelcome names by their opponents. Ideological terms like *communism* and *Marxism* may now be passé, but many of their utopian ideas have been reassigned to ideologies that have tended to minimize class struggle in favor of categories like race and sexual preference, self-consciously rebranding under the name *progressivism*.

But another, more recent term may better illustrate the problems of ideology. This word is wokeism.

The term *woke* is simply the past tense of the verb "wake," and has been used since at least as early as the 1940s by black Americans who wanted others to wake up to the idea of racial injustice.[9] Today's woke movement tends to emphasize the need to radically transform our current system to account for past and current problems of various kinds. Some people who disagree with the "woke" perspective today may worry that the invitation to "wake up" has an ulterior motive of cultural revolution akin to Marxism, but rooted in bodily characteristics or behavior instead of economic class. People who paint their opponents as espousers of wokeism are often concerned about the re-definition of every aspect of society, through the lens of not only race, but also sex, sexual identity, and sexual preference. For example, opponents of wokeism (i.e. the "anti-woke") may disagree with the narrative of race relations represented by the 1619 Project or Black Lives

Matter, and they may also be concerned with the abortion agenda of Planned Parenthood and disapprove of LGBTQ Pride Month.

Waking up to wokeism may really just be a reimagining of Marx's assertion of a timeless struggle between those with power and those without. Thus, wokeism is an ideology in the classic sense, if not *the* predominant ideology at work in the world today. Indeed, like scientism, wokeism has become a religion, with its own slogans, rituals, and leaders. Matthew Petrusek describes it as "the power to advance your political goals simply by incanting a spell-like litany of endlessly-ambiguous terms that supply immediate and unquestionable moral supremacy."[10]

What . . . No Catholicism?

Here we come at last to the question of ideology and the Catholic Church. And my contention that the Church fits into no ideological boxes, and is not an ideological box of its own, begins with one important fact that too often goes unnoticed: the word "Catholicism" is not in the *Catechism of the Catholic Church*. Nor is the word in any of the documents from the Second Vatican Council. Nor is it in any official Catholic document. Rather, to the Catholic Church, Catholicism does not officially exist.

Why?

Like the story of Israel in the Old Testament, the story of the Church is about not the triumph of a way of thinking, but the embrace of a way of life. The Church is not a way to navigate reality, but rather the experience of reality.

The Church is not a collection of ideas to lay atop human society, but the organization of humanity—the Greek word translated as Church, *ekklesia*, literally means an assembly or a gathering. To "unbox" it means to look at the whole of

human history and all of the world's people. Church teachings, then, are not the prescription for curing damnation for
the individual, but the description of life in the kingdom of
heaven for the people who belong to Christ. This kingdom
will come in full on the Last Day, and it will have no end,
but it has already come near in the person of Christ and by
the inspiration of the Holy Spirit, who communes with the
people of God in the sacraments.

Let me return to my origin story to explain further.

As I mentioned, my family was conservative and non-ideo-
logical, patriotic and Christian. But sadly, like too many
typical American families, ours fell apart shortly after I wrote
that adolescent editorial in favor of the Republican incumbent
president. As awful as the experience was, and as painful as the
memory continues to be, I give thanks for God's providence
in using my family tragedy to draw me closer to the Church,
despite its flaws (and mine). Here's the tale.

The first time I entered a medieval cathedral, I could not
imagine the whole universe containing more within it than
I found in that one building.

That building was called Notre Dame—not the one in
Paris, but rather a less famous but hardly less beautiful one in
Reims (pronounced "Rance"), about a hundred miles east of
Paris in the Champagne region of France. Reims Cathedral
was built on the site where Clovis, the Frankish king, was
baptized on Christmas Day in the year 508, and it now sits
on a lovely square, dominating the view from anywhere in
the area. On the day we were there, it was sunny and mild
outside, but the real pleasure was inside the walls.

My parents had separated one year before I set foot inside
Reims Cathedral. My sister Mary Anne and I had gone un-
accompanied to Europe to visit our father, who was at that
time stationed in Gaeta, Italy. I was fourteen, and she was

twelve. We were both at the most awkward phase of human development. Our young lives were in turmoil. I was terrified of leaving my mother, terrified of spending time with a father I didn't know very well, terrified of life and looking for answers.

I am grateful God found me that summer before an ideology could win my heart instead.

That June, our father drove us straight from Italy to France in his secondhand Mercedes-Benz diesel. The car was past its prime, but Dad had bought it specifically because it was larger and safer than most European cars. It was like a tank. He wanted to take care of us in his way, which was unfamiliar to us. He had socked away money all year to prepare for the trip of a lifetime. He was in a lot of pain and was looking for some relief. He had spent part of his own childhood in Europe, and he wanted us to experience some of what had animated his young life. Dad was not Catholic, but he knew that the most important stops on any European sightseeing tour were the sacred buildings where the Faith had been practiced for centuries—cathedrals, abbeys, basilicas, and parish churches.

During the course of our stay with our father that summer, we rode in the big yellow car not only to the cathedrals of Notre Dame in Reims and Paris, but also to Sacré-Cœur, countless baroque churches in Bavaria, the Duomo in Florence, and St. Peter's Basilica in Rome. My terror subsided as we cruised through 4,000 miles of European roads, bridges, and tunnels. For most of the time, the sun was bright above us, and the sky was blue. At night, we saw stars from a different angle from the one we knew back home. We ate *croque monsieur* and *Wienerschnitzel* and real Italian pizza that was nothing like what we were used to. Our world became much bigger than it had ever been. And it all made sense in a space just under 14,000 square feet.

Inside the walls of my first cathedral, I caught sight of where I belonged. I came in from outside, looked up at the 125-foot ceiling, and thought it went all the way to heaven. I looked around at the stained-glass windows and caught a glimpse of the uncreated Light whose will had created me and whose love was sustaining me, even in my tumultuous adolescent years. What I experienced that summer was the first beckoning of a spiritual home in the Catholic Church.

For on-the-road entertainment, my father had two cassette tapes that had probably belonged to the car's previous owner. (This was long before the days of ubiquitous electronic devices.) One was Viennese waltzes, and the other had Tom Jones on one side and Engelbert Humperdinck on the other. We quickly memorized all the '70s kitsch and got bored. So we talked, stared out the windows, and read a lot of books. Among the books that I brought with me that summer were volumes that I keep close to me even now: J.R.R. Tolkien's *Lord of the Rings* and C.S. Lewis's *Chronicles of Narnia*, which I mentioned in the Introduction. For a precocious young person whose life has been turned upside-down, there are few more reassuring places to go than the created worlds of Middle Earth and Narnia.

And so I was on a journey that summer, literally and metaphorically. I was part of a fellowship that predated my birth by many hundreds of years, that had produced the greatest works of art known to humanity, and that had given people all over the planet a meaningful existence and an eternal reward.

Bigger on the Inside

It was late in our summer sojourn that I reached the end of Lewis's last installment of the Narnia series, *The Last Battle*. I found there a beautiful invitation to an even deeper reality than I had thought possible—to an enormous imaginative space inside an already large fictional structure that Lewis had put inside seven slim, illustrated books that any child could read and understand.

In Lewis's story, a seemingly very large world comes to an end as another one that seems at first very small beckons everyone in. Old characters and new, creatures thought to be good and creatures thought to be bad, are invited into a barn door. One of the main characters, Queen Lucy, puts the new reality in a perspective that humans like you and me can understand: "In our world too, a stable once had something inside it that was bigger than our whole world."[11] Lucy is obviously referring to the incarnation of God in the nativity of Jesus Christ.

What I knew by instinct but not by intellect on that visit to Reims Cathedral in 1994 was that something dwelled in that space that was bigger than the world. I assumed for many years, after many more visits to other famous churches and holy sites, that what made the space immense was something purely indescribable and personal. But that is not the way reality works. What is, *is*. And what was present in the Cathedral of Notre Dame in Reims, just like in a little parish church in the middle of nowhere, is the Lord himself in the Blessed Sacrament. It's not just his ideas or his prescription for a better world. Indeed, in one way, a great cathedral exists for great reasons—to awe visitors with the truth, beauty, and goodness of the living God. But in another way, and more importantly, it exists to house the Lord—to keep him safe from the elements and to give the faithful a place to adore him.

Many people may recognize the motif of "bigger on the inside" not from Lewis's *Last Battle*, which was published in 1956, but in the cult British science fiction show *Doctor*

Who, which first aired in 1963. *Doctor Who* is not a Christian program, but its eponymous main character, the Doctor, is without a doubt a Christ-like figure. He comes to earth from the heavens in order to do seemingly miraculous, beneficial things throughout the universe. In one episode, called "The Satan Pit," he even battles the devil on a remote planet on the edge of a black hole.

The Doctor has a soft spot for the human race, and he has a special vocation as an agent of transformation. He saves people. In the show, fortunes are always reversed and discoveries made. The Doctor does not die, and he is able to manipulate both time and space inside his T.A.R.D.I.S. ("time and relative dimension in space"), a vehicle that looks like an old-fashioned blue telephone box once used by the police. Like the barn in Lewis's Narnia, it is bigger on the inside. And because it can travel through time and space, it opens doors to an expanded reality in ways that its external appearance would never suggest. Here is a box worth exploring!

I have been a fan of *Doctor Who* since it was resurrected by the BBC in 2005, although its more recent obsession with pushing a progressive social agenda have made it unwatchable now—that is, it has become too ideological, and it has suffered in quality because of it! But at its best, the show almost unwittingly invites us "further up and further in," as we hear in *The Last Battle*.

Life with the Doctor in the T.A.R.D.I.S. is an adventure in reality that turns out to be far more mysterious and expansive than the cleverest scientists on earth could possibly describe. Catholics know that it is only those who are wise in the Faith who have language for such vastness. In the same way, the Doctor and his T.A.R.D.I.S. give Christians a talking point for describing the thing I experienced as a teenager setting foot in a medieval house of prayer: faith is so much bigger than you could possibly imagine. Every worldly ideology seems puny in comparison.

Since Our Lord founded a new people on the rock of St. Peter, it has been the Church—the Catholic Church—that has guarded, championed, and passed on this infinitely large faith, which may appear to outsiders to be just another ideology.

I am a lifelong Christian, but when I finally made the leap into the Catholic Church at the beginning of 2019, it was nothing like crossing a small stream to go from one shifting bank to a slightly more stable one. Nor was it a question of upgrading ideology. Rather, it was climbing into the T.A.R.D.I.S. It was entering a magic barn at the end of the world. It was being both in that medieval cathedral of Reims in all its splendor and halfway across the world in a modest parish church at the same time. It was standing at the intersection of heaven and earth.

Something I had no clue about as I stood in that magnificent French cathedral as a fourteen-year-old is the thing that brings me tears of joy now. We get not only great buildings that house the Lord. We get not only a rich spiritual heritage. Indeed, these buildings and this history are the indispensable setting for this fact: we get the Lord himself. This is ultimately the greatest thing about being Catholic. We not only commune with his presence in a sacred space, but also take his nature upon us in baptism and take his body, blood, soul, and divinity into our bodies and souls when we partake of the Blessed Sacrament. We look like frail, ordinary sinners, but we are much more. As St. Paul tells the Ephesians, we are "filled with all the fullness of God" (3:19).

With all this grandeur in mind, it's hard for me, at least, to have much interest remaining in -isms. But this is not to say that Catholics must shun -isms altogether. A Catholic might embrace vegetarianism, for example, or veganism, or any number of other -isms related to food, drink, health, fitness, or leisure activities But be careful about *committing* to them. As you can see, Catholics are simply bigger on the inside. Ideologies are just too small for us.

Chapter 2

The Denomination Box

"The Roman Catholic Church, often simply referred to as the Catholic Church, is the largest Christian denomination in the world."[12] So says ChatGPT, a popular artificial intelligence resource that answers questions with astonishing, human-like clarity. In this case, the AI's answer certainly is human-like and clear . . . but it is also completely wrong.

It's really a funny thought, "denomination."

According to *The New Shorter Oxford English Dictionary*, the word *denomination* comes from the Latin *denominatio*, which, by the middle of the seventeenth century, came to mean "a body of people classed together under the one name." The same dictionary offers an early literary example of its usage from Sir Walter Scott, who wrote, "Gypsies, jockies, or cairds . . . by all these denominations such banditti were known."

Not exactly a word that conveys holiness!

Nowadays, *denomination* appears primarily in two contexts: money and church. As for the former, the use of paper money and coins is now receding into the distant memory of people raised before ubiquitous electronic commerce. But there are still a few of us alive who remember cashing a check or withdrawing money from our account and being asked by a bank teller, "What denominations would you like that in?"

Likewise, many of us have been conditioned to think of "withdrawing" from the "bank of Christianity": "Catholic? Episcopalian? Assemblies of God? What denomination would you like that in?"

Same Difference

In the 1988 comedy *Big*, Josh Baskins, played by Tom Hanks, is a kid in the body of a grown-up. After two weeks on the job as a computer programmer, he goes to the bank to cash his first paycheck, and he requests payment in the form of three dimes, a hundred-dollar bill, and eighty-seven ones—a creative array of denominations. The teller is initially surprised by her customer's juvenile monetary preference, but she fulfills his request. Nowadays, using cash is a rarity, but when it was the normal way of receiving or spending money, it made no difference to a bank or a business what combination of coins and bills a person used. The important thing was how it all added up.

The same thinking has largely affected the way people regard Christianity. And in the case of churches, there are far more options than the various combinations of legal tender. Although it is hard to precisely count the number of Christian denominations, it is safe to number them in at least the thousands. If we were to allow for a moment that the Catholic Church could be considered a denomination (spoiler: it cannot), then ChatGPT would be right: the Catholic Church is by far the largest collection of Christians, with about 1.3 billion members across the globe. Even in the United States, where Catholicism has always been a minority Christian group compared to the combined presence of the many Protestant groups, the Roman Catholic Church is nonetheless the single biggest. As recently as 2014, when the Pew Research Center published its landmark Religious Landscape Study,[13] about 20 percent of the American population identified as Roman Catholic.

With so much variety among self-identified Christians, how do we make sense of who is right and who is wrong? Are there better and worse Christian boxes? In my experience, concerns about denominationalism tend to play out in two different ways.

The first way we might call the *radical*, or even *puritanical* mentality. Looking at the Pew Research data, we notice that 2.1 percent of Americans identify as Baptists of the "Mainline" tradition, whereas 9.2 percent of Americans identify as Baptists of the "Evangelical" tradition. Within the Baptists of the Evangelical tradition, the group further divides into at least seven sub-groups, the largest of which is the Southern Baptist Convention, which in 2014 claimed 5.3 percent of the American population.

Now, it is outside our interest here to explore the doctrinal variations among these many groups that call themselves Baptist, so suffice it to say that these different groups do not normally exist as complements to one another. In fact, they often reject one another as wayward, impure alternatives. A joke by the American comedian Emo Philips illustrates the point:

> Once I saw this guy on a bridge about to jump. I said, "Don't do it!" He said, "Nobody loves me." I said, "God loves you. Do you believe in God?"
>
> He said, "Yes."
>
> I said, "Are you a Christian or a Jew?" He said, "A Christian." I said, "Me, too! Protestant or Catholic?" He said, "Protestant." I said, "Me, too! What franchise?" He said, "Baptist." I said, "Me, too! Northern Baptist or Southern Baptist?" He said, "Northern Baptist." I said, "Me, too! Northern Conservative Baptist or Northern

Liberal Baptist?" He said, "Northern Conservative Baptist." I said, "Me, too! Northern Conservative Baptist Great Lakes Region, or Northern Conservative Baptist Eastern Region?" He said, "Northern Conservative Baptist Great Lakes Region." I said, "Me, too! Northern Conservative Baptist Great Lakes Region Council of 1879, or Northern Conservative Baptist Great Lakes Region Council of 1912?" He said, "Northern Conservative Baptist Great Lakes Region Council of 1912."

I said, "Die, heretic!" And I pushed him over.[14]

Philips's story is all the funnier by his use of the word "franchise," intensifying the worldly, commercial aspect of church participation that the word *denomination* conveys. We can almost imagine using a word like "brand" or even "flavor" instead, but with eternal consequences for preferring Adidas to Nike or vanilla ice cream to chocolate.

Ecumenical Matters

On the other side—what we might call the more liberal perspective—denominations are, for the most part, brands or flavors of religion that are *merely* individual inclinations. There are some differences among groups, and some of them seem stranger to one group than another, but there is a presumption that it all washes out in the end. Church is church, just like how money is money and ice cream is ice cream.

This view of denominationalism tends to draw a caricature of *ecumenism*, which is the study of reconciling differing Christian groups. The ecumenical movement has sought to transcend what its proponents may consider insignificant or at least second-order ecclesiastical differences in pursuit of a greater spiritual unity among the baptized. The error has too often been to pit the goal of unity against the obstacle of truth. In the Catholic Church, however, truth and unity are flip sides of the same coin.

In 1948, 350 groups came together to form the World Council of Churches, whose stated objective is "striving together to realize the goal of visible Church unity."[15] In a landmark document from 1982 called "Baptism, Eucharist, Ministry," the WCC set out to breach the gaps among "divided churches" by agreeing on basic practices of Christian life. It should be noted that the Catholic Church has never been a member of the WCC and did not sign on to the final form of "Baptism, Eucharist, Ministry." The Catholic Church did welcome the document, but the American delegation tasked with responding to it also concluded that "a prerequisite for the restoration of eucharistic sharing is the satisfactory articulation of our apostolic faith."[16] That is, we cannot "agree to disagree" on any part of truth. God's revelation does not come in denominations.

In recent years, various Protestant groups—mostly of the more progressive ilk—have formed agreements to recognize one another's ministries and even exchange clergy. With the Porvoo Agreement of 1992, for example, the Church of England entered into a "full communion" relationship with several other European Protestant communities, including the official Lutheran bodies of Norway and Sweden. In the United States, the Episcopal Church entered a full-communion relationship with the Evangelical Lutheran Church in America in 2001. However, other conservative Anglican and Lutheran groups have, before and since, declared themselves out of fellowship with the Episcopal Church and the ELCA. Denominations come and go, come together, and break apart. Such is the long factionalist march from Martin Luther's Ninety-five Theses in 1517 to the present day.

Arguably even the "nondenominationalism" so prevalent now among Evangelical Protestants ultimately takes the shape of the two versions of denominationalism described above. Conservative congregations whose theological pedigree is Southern Baptist, or something like it, function like a denomination unto themselves, planting churches and forming networks. In the most extreme case, the members of an individual church building may believe that they and no one else on earth will be saved! And progressive nondenominational congregations go the other way: no denomination is needed, because any individual church building is as good as any other.

Just One of the Guys

I want to point out how it is nothing short of a miracle that the Catholic Church ever came to be considered one of the respectable religious options—a denomination—at least in the United States. In fact, for centuries, the one thing that hundreds and then thousands of Christian groups could all agree upon was that they were *not* Roman Catholic. For them, the Catholic Church was a large box from which truth had long been excluded, and which should no longer be opened at any cost. The umbrella term for most of them, "Protestant," rather says it all.

The founder of the Reformation, Martin Luther, came to believe that the pope was the Antichrist, and this view became a *de facto* principle across most Protestant traditions. When Thomas Cranmer, the first Protestant archbishop of Canterbury, went to the stake during England's brief return to Catholicism, when Queen Mary was on the throne, he declared, as the flames were about to engulf him, "As for the pope, I refuse him, as Christ's enemy and Antichrist, with all his false doctrine." Many of the original pilgrim colonists to America were Puritans—that is, non-conformists to official Church of England teachings—followed by the next waves of colonists, who were respectable Anglicans.

Whatever differences these two groups might have had, both were decidedly not interested in making common cause with Catholics or respecting their beliefs and practices as another denomination to choose from in the New World.

Of course, French and Spanish Catholics were all over the interior of the North American continent, but in the early days of the United States of America, the most significant English-speaking Catholic populations were secluded mostly in Maryland and Kentucky. Many prominent American leaders, including George Washington, promoted toleration of Catholics, and Catholics were soon granted official legal rights, but as more Catholic immigrants began coming to the United States from Europe throughout the early nineteenth century, nativist anti-Catholic sentiment hit a fever pitch. There were even a few high-profile anti-Catholic riots in Philadelphia, New York, and other population centers on the East Coast.

By the early twentieth century, the United States was a big country and getting bigger, and in some circles, Catholic missionaries like Jacques Marquette in the Midwest and Junípero Serra in California began to stand out as respectable founding-father types. Many American Protestants had moved a significant distance away from assuming that Catholics were governed by the Antichrist or had values completely at odds with the spirit of democracy.

When the United States formally entered World War I in 1917, the European powers had already been battling for years, and America's participation was much shorter in duration and far smaller in terms of personnel and losses. Nonetheless, World War I was a big deal for America. According to the Veterans Administration, the total number of U.S. service-members serving in World War I worldwide amounted to more than 4.7 million, with well over 100,000 casualties.[17]

Although at the start of World War I, most of the Catholic population of the United States consisted of recent immigrant populations that tended to remain neutral on American foreign policy, the Knights of Columbus, along with various Catholic bishops, encouraged Catholics to help the war effort. In the end, nearly one million Catholics served in the war—an extraordinarily high percentage of a total Catholic population of about 17 million.[18] Naturally, they fought alongside Protestant and Jewish Americans and forged bonds that would remain strong when they came home.

In 1928, Al Smith became the first Catholic nominated as a major party's candidate for president when the Democrats chose him to face Republican Herbert Hoover. And although Smith lost, his prominence led to a springtime for Catholic politics, which would inform a significant portion of President Roosevelt's New Deal coalition in the 1930s.

But it was World War II that brought Catholics and the Catholic Church fully into the mainstream in the United States.

For one thing, the flow of Catholic immigrants to America significantly slowed down in the 1920s and 1930s, allowing the existing Catholic communities time and space to assimilate. When World War II began, there was no question among most Catholics about where their loyalties lay: they were proud American patriots.

Moreover, unlike the relatively modest number of total American service members in World War I, in World War II, over 16 million Americans served in the war worldwide, with an estimated Catholic participation of 25 to 35 percent, or between 4 and 5.6 million Catholic personnel.[19] The war was much longer for the United States than the Great War had been, and when America's troops returned home, everyone was poised for peace, prosperity, and domestic unity.

With the glaring exception of ongoing problems with race relations, post-World War II America began to focus on what united its people. For the first time, Catholics not only were included, but took a prominent place among the "many" that formed the "one." The election of America's first Catholic president, the Harvard-educated war hero John Fitzgerald Kennedy, sealed the deal in 1960.

Popular opinion went like this: With so much to celebrate in the United States, why let religion continue to divide people? Jewish people began to integrate into American life like never before. And among Christians, denominationalism was the perfect way to maintain social cohesion despite what had often seemed like intractable differences. In this context, America began to enjoy its highest levels of churchgoing in its history—before or since—with church membership growing even faster than the fast-growing population during the Baby Boom. Buoyed by the new medium of television, the Protestant evangelist Billy Graham became a household name. And on the Catholic side, there was Fulton Sheen.

Tolerance

I often note that all four of my Protestant grandparents liked Fulton Sheen, and I am told that my Pennsylvania-German Lutheran grandmother on my father's side admired him most of all. Sheen, who had spent years being educated in Europe, was an ardently patriotic American, and despite his episcopal regalia, which none of my grandparents had likely ever seen before, he conveyed a strong sense of being just another charismatic leader in an era of good feelings. Sheen loved God, hated communism, and believed in the basic decency of people. So did my grandparents, and so did most Americans, whether Catholic, Protestant, or Jewish.

Sheen never diminished the unique truth claims of the Catholic Church—just the opposite—but he knew his audience. He did not advocate for denominationalism, but he seemed content in a system that guaranteed freedom of religion for *thee* as much as for *me*.

In an episode of his hit television show *Life Is Worth Living* called "Tolerance," Sheen's genius is right at home in the milieu of post-war America in the early 1950s. He first lightens the mood with a joke about two Irishmen named Murphy and Kelly—a hat tip to the mainstream acceptance of Catholics in American life—and then proposes a silly exercise: swap the word "tolerance" for "love." For example, if I say to my wife, "I tolerate you so much," it isn't going to go down well.

In one way, therefore, tolerance is absurd. We like what we like, and we don't like what we don't like. That goes for our religious practices as much as anything else. But in another way, Sheen argues, tolerance is an essential and praiseworthy component of a society like the United States. He notes:

> We have to tolerate the opinion of others. We may not agree with them; we may think they are very wrong; we may even think their opinion is evil. But, granted that it is, great patience and forbearance should be practiced because they are entitled to assert their own point of view.[20]

Sheen then points out the limits of tolerance, further emphasizing democratic values. "The limit of tolerance is reached," he tells us, "when tolerance would deprive someone of sovereign inalienable rights." From there, Sheen gives a brilliant tutorial on love of God and neighbor to which few if any American Christians—from the most ardent to most skeptical—could offer any objection.

No doubt, many Americans were in a position to consider the Catholic Church seriously because of Sheen's media ministry. Making the Church as much a part of American life as anything else in a transition period when the country began to understand itself as the opinion-maker for the whole world has, no doubt, had effects we can hardly measure. My own anecdote about coming from a thoroughgoing Protestant family on all sides and now raising my own Catholic children is not a great cultural rarity anymore. And yet, I have sometimes found that people's acceptance of my being Catholic is rooted in a tolerance conditioned by decades of live-and-let-live denominational thinking. One group is as good as another, the implicit logic goes, so if you find a better fit in the Catholic Church than in the Episcopal Church, more power to you. Love God, love neighbor . . . you're good.

Now again, as a "convert" (more on that word later in the book), I am grateful that I can truly flourish as a Catholic without feeling judged, or worse, being ostracized by family and friends who do not themselves believe all of the Catholic Church's teachings. For many Catholics, a day-to-day acceptance of our beliefs through others' use of a denominational mindset of "tolerance" may be good enough to keep the peace with the people we love.

But we must never finally think of ourselves or accept the designation of being just one option among others. Too much blood has been spilled by the martyrs of the past and the present for any Catholic to capitulate to the idea that our faith is just one expression of authentic Christian identity. The Catholic Church is a total vision of reality, and I want to set the tone for the rest of our study in this book by looking closely at that vision now.

Restoring the House

In 1964, Pope Paul VI issued the Second Vatican Council's "Decree on Ecumenism," called *Unitatis Redintegratio*, which translates from Latin to "The Restoration of Unity." Right there, we see that the whole notion of denominationalism is wrong. And to their credit, the mostly Protestant thinkers involved in the "Baptism, Eucharist, Ministry" document from the World Council of Churches would agree. As *most* Christians—not just Roman Catholics—profess in the Nicene Creed, the Church is "one." As *Unitatis Redintegratio* puts it plainly,

> Christ the Lord founded one Church and one Church only. However, many Christian communions present themselves to men as the true inheritors of Jesus Christ; all indeed profess to be followers of the Lord but differ in mind and go their different ways, as if Christ himself were divided. Such division openly contradicts the will of Christ, scandalizes the world, and damages the holy cause of preaching the gospel to every creature (1).

St. Paul makes the same point several times in his New Testament letters. Toward the beginning of his first letter to the Corinthians, he asks, "Is Christ divided? Was Paul crucified for you? Or were you baptized in the name of Paul?" (1:13). We may pause for a moment here to recall the prominent ecclesial bodies identified by the names of their founders, Lutherans and Calvinists chief among them. *Unitatis Redintegratio* explains,

> Even in the beginnings of this one and only Church of God there arose certain rifts, which the Apostle strongly condemned. But in subsequent centuries much more serious dissensions made their appearance and quite large communities came to be separated from full communion with the Catholic Church—for which, often enough, men of both sides were to blame (3).

To put it bluntly: Not only is the Catholic Church not a denomination, but there is no such thing as denominations. Nowhere in the Catholic Church's teaching documents will you ever find that word. You will, however, find the word *communion*, and baptized individuals and groups are connected in various degrees of communion. Another document from Vatican II—a monumental one—explains the hows and whys.

Released to the world on the same day as *Unitatis Redintegratio*, the Second Vatican Council's Constitution on the Church, *Lumen Gentium*, begins with a startlingly universal claim: "Christ is the Light of nations." When the Church begins the discussion about what it is, therefore, the emphasis is on evangelism and universality. The focus is outward. Everyone on earth was made by God and belongs in communion with God. And so, the Church asserts, the light Christ brought into the world is "brightly visible on the countenance of the Church" (1), and through the Church, "his plan was to raise men to a participation in the divine life" (2). Moreover, through communion with God, individuals, cultures, and countries throughout time are called to communion with one another as "a people made one with the unity of the Father, the Son, and the Holy Spirit" (4).

The twentieth-century theologian Henri de Lubac expresses it like this: "The unity of the mystical body of Christ, a supernatural unity, supposes a previous natural unity, the unity of the human race."[21] Note once again, the mystical body is not something to which Christians hope to be joined one day; rather, it is the sign that Christ's kingdom has already come near (Luke 17:20-21), and that the Holy Spirit has indeed descended to comfort us as Christ promised (John 15:26). Accordingly, the Church's members, by their baptism, *really* participate in the fullness of life with Christ right now.

And here we come to one of the most important first-halves of a sentence ever written, again from *Lumen Gentium*: "The Church constituted and organized in the world as a society, subsists in the Catholic Church, which is governed by the successor of Peter and by the bishops in communion with him . . ." (8). We shall look at the equally important second half of the sentence in a moment—but first, a word about *subsisting*.

Subsistence

In common parlance, the term *subsist* usually connotes the maintenance or survival of someone or something at a minimal level. A subsistence farmer is someone who grows just enough food to meet his own needs, rather than growing more to sell or trade. If one thing subsists inside another thing, then we can say it is absolutely guaranteed to live there in the full measure required, but there may be more elsewhere.

Christ's body cannot be divided and live. But Christ's body can be fully at home in one place and yet also extend its limbs far outside the boundaries of that place. Moreover, inasmuch as the body of Christ spreads out beyond the Catholic Church, its essential characteristics remain right where they have always been, unchanged. Again, *subsist*.

Now we must ask, if the Catholic Church is not a denomination and, in fact, there is no such thing from the Catholic perspective as denominations, then what are non-Roman Catholic Christians? Here we come to the second half of that all-important sentence from *Lumen Gentium*: ". . . many elements of sanctification and of truth are found outside of [the Church's] visible structures."

Non-Catholics Are Catholics?

Let us first address one big category of non–Roman Catholics: the Eastern Orthodox.

In the early days of Christianity, the Church functioned more like a collection of churches, often using different liturgies and worshiping in different languages, but sharing the same faith at the core of unity across differences. The bishop of Rome, whose church was well known for its orthodoxy, inherited the identity given by Christ to Peter—namely, the living authority over all Christians.

Sadly, over the course of some decades, many of the churches of the Greek-speaking "East," centered in Constantinople, declared themselves out of communion with the pope in Rome, effecting a tragic separation known today as the Great Schism. The year assigned to this "event" is usually 1054, when the patriarch of Constantinople and the pope's legate excommunicated each other, but the Great Schism had been brewing long before that exchange and took years after it to become concrete.

The Eastern churches tended to have a different understanding from that of the West with regard to the ministry of the pope, the pattern of church governance, the type of bread to use in the Holy Eucharist, and various other tensions. One particularly thorny crisis came over the Eastern churches' objection to the Roman church's use of the term *filioque*, or "and with the Son," when teaching the Church's view on the Holy Spirit. The Roman church taught that the Holy Spirit proceeds from the Father *and* the Son, but the Eastern churches pointed out that the original version of the Nicene Creed said only "from the Father." Almost one thousand years ago, East and West parted ways, giving rise to the Eastern Orthodox churches on the one side and the Catholic Church on the other side.

The Catholic Church does recognize Eastern Orthodox sacraments and thus considers these Eastern churches real churches. This makes unity—participating together as one in true worship, as Jesus Christ intended—all the more crucial. In his landmark encyclical letter on ecumenism from 1994, called *Ut Unum Sint*, Pope St. John Paul II expressed his hope for eventual reunion between West and East, saying, "The Church must breathe with her two lungs!" (54).

The situation for Protestants is a little different.

At the time of the Reformation in Europe in the early sixteenth century, there was a real and lasting break on the part of a significant number of Christians in Europe with their sacramental heritage in the Roman Catholic Church. In Lutheranism, Calvinism, Anglicanism, and the many hundreds of groups that soon proliferated, there was no longer a sacramental priesthood, and there was no longer unity among believers centered in the living authority of the pope. People who professed Christ crucified, risen, and glorified were not fully nourished with the grace of Christ in all of the Church's sacraments.

And yet, every person baptized in the name of the Father, and of the Son, and of the Holy Spirit has a real connection to the beating heart of the true faith. Again, the body of Christ *subsists in* the Catholic Church, but Christ has not totally abandoned the part of his flock wandering outside the gates of his fold. The Second Vatican Council helpfully supplies the language to describe these sheep: "separated brethren" (*Lumen Gentium* 67 and 69, *Unitatis Redintegratio* 1 and following). As St. Paul frequently referred to the faithful with the same term, "brethren" or "brothers and sisters," it is highly significant that Catholics are taught to regard non-Catholic Christians in this way. That is, Protestants are not *something* else (we're all Christians!), but they are *somewhere* else (in a different or lesser degree of communion).

So, although it may sound slightly patronizing to a Protestant, Catholics basically believe that there is not really any other way to be a Christian besides being Catholic. An individual or a group that "protests" some or even most things the Catholic Church teaches is not nothing, but it is not everything. And a special task of Catholics is not to content ourselves with separation under the guise of denominationalism. Rather, again in the words of *Unitatis Redintegratio*, "we must get to know the outlook of our separated brethren" (9).

Lead Kindly, Newman

Let us briefly examine the outlook of a once-separated (and also once very famous) brother, John Henry Newman, whom I discussed briefly in the Introduction. In Newman's day and place, people did not use the term *denomination*; rather, they recognized an established Protestant church, the Church of England, and tolerated many other "nonconformist" Protestant groups. There were, of course, Catholics, too. The variety of Christianity was so extensive in England that the French *philosophe* Voltaire quipped, "England has forty-two religions and only two sauces."

Anyway, Newman was an Anglican clergyman and scholar whose decision to become a Catholic in 1845 prefigured the problem of denominationalism. Newman described his journey in his 1864 spiritual memoir, *Apologia Pro Vita Sua*. In this book, Newman tells us that by the year 1839, he had reached a crossroads. For a long while, he was content to believe that his English forebears had disfigured the truth but had not destroyed it. Maybe the Church was more like a tree, and his own ecclesiastical group was an authentic branch. Maybe he could remain out on a limb, but also belong *fully* to the body of Christ without becoming a Catholic.

But Newman was a scholar of antiquity, and in particular, he was an expert on the theological controversies of
the first few centuries of Christianity. In all his searching,
he could never uncover evidence that the one Church that
Christ founded was ever meant to grow out from different
branches with a common trunk. Again, people did not really
talk about "denominations" back then, but Newman could
not find anything in history that justified maintaining different groups of Christians who were not in full communion
with one another.

For Newman's part, his rejection of something like a na-
scent denominationalism came from his intense consider-
ation of the groups that emerged in the aftermath of various early Church councils. He reflected on his experience
reading about a particular group called the Monophysites,
or "one-nature people." This group believed everything the
Church taught up until the Council of Chalcedon in the
year 451, which defined Christ as having two natures—one
fully God and one fully man, united in one person, but not
mixed together.

As an Anglican, Newman most certainly accepted the
ancient teaching of the two natures of Christ. He was no
Monophysite, but he saw in the story of the Monophysites an
analogy for himself and for his ecclesiastical tribe. He wrote,
"My stronghold was Antiquity; now here, in the middle of
the fifth century, I found, as it seemed to me, Christendom
of the sixteenth and nineteenth centuries reflected. I saw my
face in that mirror, and I was a Monophysite."[22]

Newman knew that he was not nothing, but that he was
not everything. It took him six more years to finally take the
leap into the Catholic Church, and once he did, he became
one of its greatest promoters and defenders in its whole cen-
turies-long history. His beautiful testimony about his decision

to come into full communion with Rome exposed the lie of denominationalism long before denominationalism would come into vogue. Would that more people had read him!

But what should we say to people who are proud of the distinct features of their own ecclesial groups and have no desire to wipe away their community's Christian legacy? Again, the Catholic Church does not leave us in the dark. In *Ut Unum Sint*, John Paul II refers to "the elements of sanctification and truth present in the other Christian communities" (11). Moreover, he says that these elements create "a recognition of the degree of communion already present" (49).

In 2009, Pope Benedict XVI instantiated his predecessor's ecumenical vision in a document called *Anglicanorum Coetibus*, which allows Anglicans to come into full communion with the Catholic Church while retaining elements of their liturgical, spiritual, and pastoral traditions. The document established "personal ordinariates," which are jurisdictions within the Catholic Church based on particular membership criteria—namely, having previously been Anglican—rather than geographical territory. Through the ordinariates, Pope Benedict explained, some former Protestants not only receive recognition of the value of some parts of their former tradition, but also can continue living within this tradition as "a treasure to be shared" with their fellow Catholics.

Finally, John Paul II reminds us that the common identity created across ecclesial boundaries in holy baptism is an enormous victory to celebrate. Additionally, Catholics and non-Catholics alike have died for the sake of Christ and his kingdom. "All these elements," the late pontiff notes, "bear within themselves a tendency toward unity, having their fullness in that unity" (14). We will soon explore the idea of "fullness" much more. Before we start, let us give thanks that we do not have to settle for partial good news confined to boxed-up traditions.

The Catholic Church is not a denomination, thanks be to God. Take that, ChatGPT.

CHAPTER 3

The Religion Box

In September 2023, Apple CEO Tim Cook released a video on social media declaring an ambitious program for the tech behemoth's elimination of carbon from its manufacturing operations. To dramatize the self-congratulatory announcement, Apple produced a skit featuring professional actors, including Academy Award-winner Octavia Spencer playing "Mother Nature."

When Mother Nature arrives, Cook asks anxiously, "How was the weather?" She stridently replies, "The weather was however I wanted it to be!" The employees then rattle off all the ways they have made progress toward the environmentalist ideals their visitor may have in her mind. But their intentions are never pure enough, nor are their efforts strong enough: Mother Nature is impossible to please. Despite assuring her of plastic-free packaging in carbon-neutral consumer goods, which have hit the market way ahead of schedule, Mother Nature stands before this group of sycophants as a parent whose children can never measure up. The implicit message is that humans are always the problem with the world. "Don't disappoint your mother," the deity declares on her way out, as everyone in the room breathes an audible sigh of relief.

One critique of the Apple skit is its lip service to environmentalism, an always vague and ever-changing ideology. Replacing the older virtues of conservation and stewardship, environmentalism prioritizes the earth itself over its suitability for humans to use what it provides to meet our needs.

As we saw in the last chapter, ideologies are boxes that inherently limit our outlook on everything, as contrasted with the holistic vision of reality proposed by the Catholic Church from generation to generation. Environmentalism is a good example of how ideology functions as religion, complete with a new god rebranded out of an old one—e.g., Mother Nature. Therefore, in this chapter, we shall build on our critique of ideology and examine the more troubling phenomenon of the proliferation of non-Christian and anti-Christian religious views, particularly by people who are avowedly non-religious.

Societies that have been Christian for a long time are now becoming pagan again, dusting off and opening up old boxes, with effects sometimes reminding us of Pandora's infamous box. The Catholic Church could try—and, some might argue, has tried—to meet this new challenge by competing for religious space in a crowded market of things to worship. Or the Church could respond by being what it has always been, not unreflectively striving to become what it cannot be—namely, a religion in competition with other religions, old and new. Indeed, Christianity as it has been experienced and taught in the Catholic Church for more than 2,000 years is more than a religion, and Catholics today should never settle for an explanation of the Faith as merely a religion, even if the best one. Instead, the Catholic faith is the revelation of God in Christ, who is all in all, and therefore the answer to all the questions of the philosophers and the only hope for healing and wholeness.

Philosophy Is Better than Religion

The religions of antiquity offered basic explanations for certain phenomena, but they had no coherent theological worldview. There was usually a hierarchy of gods, each with different powers and purviews, and they vied not only with one another for influence, but also made allies and enemies among human beings. The old gods were competitive, like humans, only inhabiting a divine space rather than an earthly one. They demanded favors, which they did not explain, and they were happy to keep their distance from people when they had no need of them or were satisfied by what they were offered. The worship of these gods required sacrifice, but the gods offered no mercy in return. Moreover, the duties of human piety were usually synonymous with the perfunctory rituals of civic life, even among the impious.

In 399 B.C., the famous ancient philosopher Socrates was given the death penalty for thinking differently about religion, the gods, and God. In Plato's *Apology*, we learn that Socrates has been brought up on charges "of corrupting the young and of not believing in the gods in whom the city believes, but in other new spiritual things." We learn more about what these "new spiritual things" are in another of Plato's dialogues, *Euthyphro*.[23]

The question at the heart of *Euthyphro* is "What is piety?" The dialogue's namesake, Euthyphro, has brought his own father up on charges of murdering a servant. In ancient Athens, both murder and betraying one's parents were considered violations of the will of the gods. So, according to the logic of ancient Athenian religion, Euthyphro should be considered just as impious for turning in his father as his father is for murdering a servant.

Justifying himself, Euthyphro notes that Zeus, "the most just of the gods," bound and castrated his father, Cronos, for swallowing his sons.[24] Socrates's interest is piqued. How can the gods themselves transgress laws of piety? And by extension, what are we to make of the gods' disagreements about basic concepts like justice, goodness, and beauty?

As usual with Plato's dialogues, the discussion between Socrates and Euthyphro ends in *aporia*, which is the word for confusion or doubt used for rhetorical effect. Nonetheless, it is easy to conclude that there must be an ultimate source of meaning beyond the gods—indeed, outside the universe itself. Right is right, and wrong is wrong. Truth transcends the gods.

Where Truth Leads

In yet another of Plato's dialogues, *Phaedo*, Socrates's conviction is at least partly related to the crime of teaching that the immortal human soul becomes one with Being itself, and therefore that there is something more powerful than the Greek pantheon.

Socrates's final words to Crito before he succumbs to hemlock poisoning are "I owe a cock to Asclepius; do not forget to pay it."[25] Asclepius was the Greek god of medicine. By remembering that he owes a sacrifice to a god, Socrates reveals his willingness to participate in pagan religion as a formality, even though he taught an ultimate reality beyond routine sacrifices. There was God, who is an altogether different being from gods. And the critical discipline of philosophy, rather than the conformist practice of civic religion, shows us the way to him.

The death of Socrates is illustrative in our study of what religion is and our assertion that the Catholic Church is something more than religion. In Socrates's teachings, preserved and expanded by his student, Plato, we see the limitations of mere religion, also known as *cult*, in light of a larger framework of transcendent truth. And just as "cult" is the root of "culture," society goes wrong when it places ultimate meaning in things that are "penultimate," or secondary to the fullness of truth. Things like environmentalism. Things like any merely civic or this-worldly religion.

Real truth—*the* truth—is always worth dying for. In Socrates's case, but also among most of the other non-Jewish peoples of antiquity, we see how the religion of the gods *per se* was not worth dying for at all. Rather, people understood that their local gods warred and wooed and consumed—in other words, did the same sorts of things they did, only on a cosmic scale. They were comfortable worshiping pagan deities as part of their duties, but no one looked to Rah or Zeus or Odin for a revelation of all truth. In fact, the best-case scenario for paganism was always that the gods would simply stay away. Think again of the relief our twenty-first-century environmentalist Apple techies express when Mother Nature finally leaves them alone.

Rather, in the ancient world, when it came to questions of ultimate meaning, it was to philosophy, not religion that people turned. Socrates says in the *Phaedo* dialogue that someone who turns to the transcendent truth of God that philosophy proposes "is probably right to be of good cheer in the face of death and to be very hopeful that after death he will attain the greatest blessings yonder."[26]

Although the Greeks were famous for philosophy, the relatively little-known people of Israel had a unique way of life that combined philosophy and liturgy in ways other religious competitors did not. One of the most important aspects of early Christianity was its natural integration of Greek and Hebrew thought and worship. Although Christianity, like Judaism, was and is a religion with initiation rites, sacrifices, prayers, priests, and holy sites, it was and is also the continuation of and fulfillment of the entire ancient philosophical tradition.

It is of the utmost importance, therefore, that when the Messiah of Israel came into the world, he was understood to be *Logos*, the incarnate Word or Reason—the God of philosophy made flesh. It was those who were real seekers after truth, represented by the three Magi from the East, who anticipated Christ even before his arrival. Therefore, as the second-century Christian philosopher Justin Martyr put it, "those who lived in accordance with Reason are Christians . . . fearless and unperturbed."[27] To see how the Catholic Church that Justin died for in A.D. 165 remains the guardian and promoter of the Word down to the present day, let us return to the question of the gods versus God.

The Old Gods and Monsters

In the Bible, there are a few instances where we see sorcerers and wonderworkers wielding real power. In the book of Exodus, for example, in the midst of the ten plagues, Moses' brother Aaron throws down his rod, which becomes a serpent in the presence of Pharaoh. Pharaoh's magicians are able to transform their rods, too, "by their secret arts" (Exod. 7:11). Likewise, Pharaoh's religious leaders can replicate turning water into blood (v. 22) and conjure up frogs (8:7). It is only with the third plague, turning dust into gnats, that the Egyptians can no longer compete. "This is the finger of God," they declare (v. 19). Even Israel's enemies recognize that the Israelite deity is of a wholly different nature from the capricious entities of everyone else's religious systems.

When really put to the test, God permits no rivals. We learn of God's omnipotence in his ultimate deliverance of Israel from Egypt through the Red Sea, but the gods of the nations persist despite being vanquished repeatedly.

The most famous of the ancient deities opposed to the God of Abraham, Isaac, and Jacob is one variety or another of Baal, the Canaanite god of weather and fertility—a Mother and Father Nature. In 1 Kings, we find the story of Baal's defeat, which leads to a long exile perhaps only recently ended. Sometime around the middle of the ninth century B.C., there reigned over Israel the notoriously wicked King Ahab, who erected a temple and an altar to Baal for his foreign wife, Jezebel. As punishment for Israel's unfaithfulness under Ahab and Jezebel, the prophet Elijah proclaimed a drought and went into hiding.

Eventually, God ordered Elijah to return to Ahab to announce God's willingness to open the skies and send rain to the earth again. Before that could happen, however, God had to display his sovereignty by sending Elijah to Mount Carmel to face "the four hundred and fifty prophets of Baal and the four hundred prophets of Asherah, who eat at Jezebel's table" (1 Kings 18:19). Unlike Aaron and Moses at Pharaoh's court, Baal's servants are completely powerless to match the wonder-working of God's servant Elijah. In shocking fashion, the failed prophets of Baal become raving mad in their impotence, mutilating themselves with sharp weapons as a symbol that all false religion ultimately leads to despair. Finally, Elijah puts them out of their misery, killing them.

The point here is not that Christians should follow Elijah's lead and kill people of other religions. Not at all. Rather, we take note that in the Bible, servants of the true God never forget that God has competition from the gods of various cults, nor do they doubt that God will ultimately subdue and dominate these errant entities. As St. Paul finally declares about God's triumph in his Messiah: "Christ is all, and in all" (Col. 3:11). On this side of God's final victory in the Second Coming, however, the weapons of God's enemies are not always without an edge, even if their effects are only temporary.

Fast-forward several centuries to the early days of Christianity, where we meet St. Augustine of Hippo, the greatest philosopher-theologian of the Patristic era.

Augustine was a zealous convert to Christ and the Church but also a lifelong admirer of Plato, trained in the highest arts of Roman rhetoric. Augustine saw the Roman Empire crumbling, and he looked out on an uncertain future, synthesizing a wide array of knowledge into the biblical imagination of a Catholic bishop. There were all sorts of religious offerings to sift through, including traditional paganism, Manicheism, various Gnosticisms, animisms, philosophical systems, syncretistic hybrids, and heretical forms of Christianity like Donatism and Pelagianism.

There was also Platonism, the expanded teachings of Socrates and Plato. But for all that Augustine admired Plato, and for all that we have demonstrated here how Socrates's philosophical worldview is more like Christianity than the ancient pagan religions, Platonism, like all -isms, is insufficient to understand all of reality.

Amid a busy and dangerous life visiting his far-flung congregations as a bishop in rural northern Africa, Augustine both diagnosed his society's ills and prescribed an abiding remedy in his monumental work *City of God*, published in the aftermath of the sack of Rome in 410. Many pagans blamed Christianity for undermining their ancient deities and compromising the common good. Augustine thought otherwise.

Augustine saw the situation quite differently from the pagan intellectual elite of his age, noting that "Rome had sunk into the dregs of the worst immorality well before the coming of our heavenly king."[28] The blame for Rome's demise lay not with the new Christian God, but with the inherent weakness of the venerable old pagan pantheon tasked with preserving the virtue of the Romans. In one place in *The City of God*, Augustine points out that the Roman scholar Varro feared that "the gods may perish, due not to any enemy invasion but to the sheer indifference of the citizens."[29]

Likewise, Augustine explains, Virgil's hero Aeneas "is said to have saved his household gods from the fall of Troy"—a telling illustration of the impotence of idols to sustain or save, since they turn out to need saving by human beings instead. But these gods are not nothing. Rather, they are real, Augustine argues, but they "are actually pernicious demons."[30] Augustine warns pagans to turn and accept the gospel, because their religion is deeply harmful both to their individual souls and to society at large. Augustine says of the pagan gods, "They are malignant spirits for whom your eternal happiness is punishment."[31]

Few people today, including devout Christians, pause to consider the possibility that the resurgence of non-Christian religion in its various forms—nature-worship, yes, but everything else from the protest rituals of wokeism to outright Satanism, too—may be a return of the demonic entities of the past. That is, non-Christian religion is not just a distraction from humans' quest for truth in the world, but a menace to their immortality. In the vacuum left by a once-Christian society that has opted for illusions of public neutrality and private faith, the old gods have kicked open the door and begun preying on our vulnerable souls as in ancient times.

"You Speak Latin?"

We find a horrific cinematic proposal about the effect of the return of the old gods in the 1973 film *The Exorcist*. Directed by William Friedkin with a screenplay adapted by William Peter Blatty from his own novel, *The Exorcist* is the story of a young girl, Regan MacNeil, whose thoroughly secular mother, Chris, a famous actress, finally realizes that demonic possession is the only explanation for her daughter's shocking and unnatural behavior. Chris finds a Jesuit priest named Damien Karras, who is also a psychiatrist, and he reluctantly agrees to investigate whether Regan may indeed be suffering from demonic possession instead of mental illness. Fr. Karras is assisted by a mysterious older priest named Fr. Lankester Merrin, and the pair are finally successful in delivering the demon from Regan, but both men die in the process.

Now, most viewers of *The Exorcist* appreciate the film as fiction, pure and simple. Demons are just one of many types of scary monsters that filmmakers put on screen to sell tickets. And Friedkin and his team of cinematic technicians used effects in *The Exorcist* never before seen in a mainstream movie, causing some theatergoers to become ill. There were even rumors that pregnant women were sent into premature labor by the trauma of watching the movie.

Some people of faith today, however, find *The Exorcist* frightening precisely because they have studied the reality of spiritual warfare. Demons are real, and the Church has the power from Christ to defeat them. But there is more to the story, and even devout Catholic viewers of *The Exorcist* miss an important plot point relevant to our navigation of today's religious landscape.

The Exorcist begins with a somewhat discordant prologue, where Merrin, played by the eminent Swedish actor Max von Sydow, discovers an ancient talisman while on an archaeological dig in northern Iraq. In writing the original novel and the subsequent screenplay, Blatty based Merrin partly on the famous French Jesuit Pierre Teilhard de Chardin, who was a Darwinian scientist and a mystic philosopher. Although Merrin does not play a large role in the film adaption, Blatty and Friedkin subtly make it clear in *The Exorcist* that Regan's possession is directly related to what the old priest unearthed and brought back to America.

In this way, *The Exorcist* is really the story of Merrin's—and, by extension, the Church's—ongoing struggle with an ancient evil long buried but not yet vanquished for good. And this evil's origin in the sands of modern Iraq points us to the ancient conquerors of the kingdoms of Israel and Judah: Assyria and Babylon—the same deity or deities that Elijah temporarily defeated on Mount Carmel in the Old Testament.

The Exorcist presents a rare worst-case scenario for a person who is vulnerable to evil influences that have remained in the world, despite the best efforts of Christians over the centuries to minimize their effects. Regan is just a kid, who does not deserve what happens to her. Nonetheless, her suffering illustrates how the old gods plague not just the people who either naïvely or maliciously invite them in. Rather, because the world is fallen, the Enemy's victims do not always bear a one-to-one correspondence to guilt or innocence.

When Jesus heals the man born blind, he rejects the premise of the question "Who sinned, this man or his parents?" (John 9:2). What matters instead is how the triumph of God's power in one person's life may be an example to the world.

All About Me

At the end of *The Exorcist*, we are left to wonder whether Regan's ordeal will turn the hearts of those around her toward the truth of Christ. But whether a person is possessed by a demon or not, and what such activity may mean in any particular case, the way we think about ourselves today is an invitation to idolatry and bad religion. After all, only at the bitter end of the quest to find out what is wrong with Regan do her mother, her doctors, and even Karras turn to the possibility that the menace lies outside Regan's own body and mind. They check all the other boxes first, and look outside ready-made answers only as a last resort. Such is our instinct in the modern West—for better or for worse, it's all about the individual experience.

On this point, St. Augustine may guide us again toward a better way—the Catholic Church's way. He can speak to us in particular from the perspective of trying to find meaning for himself, but via the philosophical method of self-criticism in light of revealed truth. Like all of us, Augustine was once blind and came to see. But unlike most of us, he described his embrace of truth in language destined to be remembered for centuries.

Backing up a couple of decades before he wrote *City of God*, we encounter in the pre-Christian Augustine a prototype of the modern Western person: smart, successful, and miserable. He has tried a variety of religions, but he is still left with the realization that he can do everything except save himself. Just before his Christian conversion in a garden in Milan, Augustine reminds us in his *Confessions*, "This debate in my heart was a struggle of myself against myself."[32] Augustine's greatest theological debate is not with a foreign opponent, but with his competing identities. He remembers his mistaken view of Christ as "a man of excellent wisdom which none could equal."[33] Jesus was important, but ultimately he was just another god to take or leave as one wished.

For a while, Augustine embraced a dualistic religion called Manicheism, which is in some ways similar to a modern mishmash of Eastern and Western spiritualities of good versus evil. Augustine ultimately found Manichaeism untenable. More miserable, he returned to philosophy and progressed to some extent toward truth. But not even Plato could take him all the way to wholeness.

Platonism did show Augustine how God's Son, who is God's wisdom, could be by nature the same thing as God himself.[34] But nowhere in the ancient Greeks did he find the definition of Christ from St. Paul's hymn in Philippians 2:6–11—the Christ who was pulling Augustine ever toward him is God *and* man, who "humbled himself being made obedient to death" and at whose name "every knee should bow." In the full revelation of Christ, therefore, we see the deficiencies of even the best philosophy, but we also recognize the truth philosophy is finally striving to find.

As we saw at the start of the chapter with the example of Apple's skit about Mother Nature, Western society is now in a crisis caused by jettisoning the totalizing vision of Christianity and turning back to mere religions. And although these religions take many guises, bringing back ancient evils and overlapping with all the *-isms* we explored in the last chapter, the self is at the center of it all. Sadly, today's obsession with self lacks the critical examination characteristic of philosophical inquiry in Socrates's famous statement from Plato's *Apology*: "The unexamined life is not worth living." To the Christian, the examined, individual life is the forum for what St. Paul calls "God's handiwork" (Eph. 2:10).

The Kids Aren't Alright

In the span of just a couple of decades, humans have become subject to a barrage of influences that turn them inward while completely jettisoning the self-critical apparatus of philosophy that turns them outward to God and neighbor. The result is the worst kind of non-philosophical religion, with individualized principles and practices detached from ultimate, universal meaning. Our late Holy Father, Pope Benedict XVI, offered an analysis of this monumental shift, and his analysis holds up even better now than when he offered it back in 2004.

On the eve of his election as pope, Cardinal Joseph Ratzinger noted in a now famous homily at Mass for the College of Cardinals that "we are building a dictatorship of relativism that does not recognize anything as definitive and whose ultimate goal consists solely of one's own ego and desires."[35] These words were controversial, and they have proved prophetic. In less than two decades, this relativism has morphed into complete atomization in Western society and a religious dictatorship of our making.

Indeed, the most pernicious religiosity these days is not merely prioritizing opinions above doctrine or refusing to commit to the one true religion over other false ones (or none). Christianity is not merely competing with the return of the demonic gods of paganism (which it is), nor is Christianity merely failing to articulate its exclusive truth claims amid other faiths and philosophies that discourage people from staking an exclusive claim (which, again, it is). Rather, social media now allow each of us to play God for himself, constructing false identities *ex nihilo* and then worshiping them in one dopamine-hit scroll after another after another.

These gods of self, like all the gods of the imposter religions, are out to destroy us.

In her illuminating 2018 book *iGen*, psychologist Jean Twenge has shared unprecedented data about loneliness, disconnection, and depression in the generation that came of age in Pope Benedict's pontificate, which corresponds to the advent of the smartphone. Between 2011 and 2015, there was a 50-percent increase in major depressive disorders among young people. The suicide rate for twelve- to fourteen-year-olds has doubled since 2007. Older generations are not immune. Even standing with thousands of other people at a sporting event, museum outing, or pilgrimage, the goal becomes capturing and customizing rather than receiving and experiencing. "Sharing" becomes a click of my finger on a screen for followers or fans "out there" rather than choosing awareness of and connection to the people standing next to me.

Today's fragmented souls need more than religion—a fact that early Christians knew well, but we have mostly forgotten. In an essay he wrote as pope emeritus, Benedict XVI pointed out this fact of the past and our need to rediscover it today. He wrote, "In the mission that developed in Christian antiquity, Christianity did not conceive of itself as a religion but, rather, in the first place as a continuation of philosophical thought, in other words, of man's search for truth."[36] Neither the civic paganism of Augustine's day nor the self-tailored online existence of the twenty-first century offers the vision of the fullness of truth that the Church describes.

Down with Promiscuity, Up with Truth

Then, there's morality. Behavior, and particularly sexual behavior, was the touchstone in Augustine's day that made Christianity seem so radically different from other religions. It still is. On the one hand, the Pew Research Center show that young people have more problems than ever with the Church's teachings about sexual morality.[37] And there are nearly as many expressions of sexual identity as there are people to express them. But on the other hand, as journalist Kate Julian demonstrated in an article in *The Atlantic* in 2018, sexual promiscuity is strangely way down among this same demographic of younger people, even as the use of pornography is way up.[38]

What a mess. But today, as in Augustine's time, only Christianity offers liberation from both promiscuity and the slavery of self-gratification, in much the same way that it offered a path out of the pagan orgies and the culture of libertinism of ancient Rome. The Church now, as then, offers "life in Christ," which is the official term the *Catechism of the Catholic Church* uses to describe morality. What Catholics hold as definitive moral teaching, therefore, is precisely not a set of arbitrary dos and don'ts.

One can almost feel the longing in people today for the will to put down their phones, individual glowing boxes, and find real connection—to know themselves, to know and be known by a lifelong spouse or remain celibate rather than jump from partner to partner or gratify themselves with pornography. Who knows how many members of a new generation of unhappy young men and women may be unwittingly praying at this moment, as Augustine once did, "Grant me chastity and continence, but not yet"?[39] And yet, eventually, Augustine discovered life in Christ as his way out of the bondage of sins of the flesh, and he therefore felt and experienced salvation even on this side of eternity. Augustine's submission to the Church not only overcame for him what he could not achieve on his own, but also taught him in the end to be himself—ironically, the purported but never-realized goal of the "dictatorship of relativism."

Neither Jupiter nor demons nor household gods nor a Manichean demiurge nor the ego nor the iPhone nor a one-sided Jesus offers to help a person become whole. Only the real Christ, God and man united, provides unity amid diversity, eschews the priority of any category of identity above "son of God," and promotes universal brotherhood and the common good. The real Christ, who is perfect God and perfect man, offers us in the Catholic Church a unity of individuality and belonging.

In the embrace of this truth, the Catholic Church can never be a mere religion. God is with us as one of us—in the Church, and not simply up there or out there or maybe somewhere. In this regard, it is important to realize that the Church as Christ founded it exists right now. The authentic Church has not ceased to be and is not waiting to come into existence in the right form. This reality makes all the difference to our lives and to the life of the world.

CHAPTER 4

The Institution Box

We get used to having certain places, events, and people in our lives. To mark the longevity and gravity of their presence, we sometimes label them "institutions."

The oldest pub in Oxford, England, The Bear, is an institution. The State Fair of Texas, complete with its Big Tex mascot, is an institution. The longest-running scripted television show in American history, *The Simpsons*, is an institution. These kinds of institutions belong to the informal understanding of tradition—something that is quasi-venerable mostly on account of its existence, but all the more if it happens to serve good ale, offer a good time for the family, or makes us laugh.

Conversely, sometimes a place, event, or person may become an institution precisely because it exists while inspiring disgust or failing to meet basic expectations over a long span of time. For example, the rats in the New York City subway are an institution.

An institution may also be a more formal and formative organization or operation: a university, a military unit, a media enterprise, a branch of government, or even a sports team. These bodies inspire loyalty or, when deficient, disappointment. These institutions aspire to levels of influence that transcend the individual, the family, or the small group, and they embody a more substantial understanding of tradition. Society depends upon these institutions' existence, and therefore their members have a responsibility to ensure their integrity. The 1978 film *National Lampoon's Animal House* demonstrates the dilemma of what to do when one of these formative institutions becomes corrupt. Should we destroy it or reform it? On the one hand, to shut down Faber College's Delta Tau Chi fraternity house would remove a meeting place for moral degeneracy (and that would be good). On the other hand, one of the fraternity's members explains, "Delta house has a long tradition of existence." It is hard to re-create a good thing from scratch once its bad version has been done away with.

Obviously, the Catholic Church has a longer tradition of existence than most things on earth. And many things about the Catholic Church are institutional in both of the senses I have described. If we "unboxed" the Church, we would certainly find things that looked like an institution.

Informally, a beloved and long-serving priest of a particular parish may become an institution. Or a town's Lenten fish dinner hosted by the Knights of Columbus may be thought of as an institution. More formally, the Catholic Church has founded and operated some of the most prestigious universities in the world. In Europe, but also in North America and elsewhere, church buildings are among the most beautiful and prominent structures in our cities and towns. Monasteries, charity organizations, advocacy groups, and so many more formal organizations, large and small, standing beneath the banner of the Catholic Church, are too numerous to list. The Catholic Church is full of institutions—*lousy with them*, as people used to say.

But the Catholic Church itself is not an institution. The basic reason why is simply put but poorly understood: human beings create institutions, whereas God created the Church.

Let us explore further by looking back to the Catholic Church's predecessor, the people of Israel.

The Temple

To the ancient Israelites, the Temple in Jerusalem was where heaven and earth met. It inspired the same sense of awe and wonder that a beautiful cathedral like the one I described in Reims or a comparable one in Ravenna or Rangoon can inspire in us today, and for the same reason: God dwelled there. The Psalms contemplate and celebrate the Temple often. The Old Testament demonstrates in various places not only how beautiful the first Temple was, but how spiritually alive it was, too, in the Ark of the Covenant, perhaps the most important box in the entire Bible (Exod. 25). The Psalmist declares, "O Lord, I love the habitation of thy house, and the place where thy glory dwells" (26:8).

Israel built the Temple because God told them to, and naturally the Temple became all-important to ancient Israelite identity—but ultimately, Judaism could and would exist without it, even without the Ark of the Covenant. That is, being Jewish was for ancient Israel synonymous with being human. And this way of life persisted even when all the institutional trappings around Israel failed: their kingdom and all its organizational apparatuses, but most importantly, the Temple itself, built by human hands.

In the year 586 B.C., the Babylonians destroyed the Temple in Jerusalem, and the people of Israel were scattered abroad. The prophet Ezekiel describes the destruction, and the Lord's departure, as a consequence of Israel's faithlessness. Nonetheless, Israel itself, and God's covenant with Israel, did not fail, as mere institutions do. No doubt, some Israelites exceeded the faithfulness of others during the time of exile, and their remnant faithfulness would later prove to be the seed of a replanted culture. Millennia later, in the twentieth century, even the diabolical Nazi war machine could not eradicate the Jews from the earth.

In the year 538 B.C., many of the people of Israel returned to their homeland and began work on a new, second Temple. The biblical books of Ezra and Nehemiah recount the story of Israel's rebuilding—not only of their Temple and cities, but of their identity as a people restored. In Ezra 10, we learn that Israelite men had to divorce their foreign wives and even disown their foreign children. Although some elements of this story may disturb us today, we see clearly in it how to Jews and later to Christians, God's revelation creates and some-times re-creates institutions, not vice versa. Israel's desire to be more than a mere political organization with a holy site is evident in Nehemiah 8, when "all the people gathered as one man" (v. 1) to hear the book of the Law read publicly for the first time in many decades. They worshiped and wept. It was time to rebuild institutions to facilitate their re-formation as a people, but the people themselves were a God-given reality.

"We Are Semites Spiritually"

At the time of Jesus, this second Temple had never looked better.

Herod the Great, whose paranoia about the birth of the king of the Jews forced the Holy Family to flee to Egypt after Jesus' birth, was a famously flawed man. But during his time serving as a puppet ruler for the Romans, he engaged in some large-scale public projects, including the renovation and expansion of the Temple at Jerusalem. In Luke's Gospel, we learn that Jesus, Mary, Joseph, and other members of Jesus' community made regular pilgrimages from Nazareth to Jerusalem to visit their spiritual home on earth. On one occasion, the adolescent Jesus wandered off from his family, found the Temple on his own, and taught in it. When Our Lady and St. Joseph finally found him, he asked them, "Did you not know that I must be in my Father's house?" (Luke 2:49).

A couple of decades later, Jesus entered the Temple with his disciples, at least some of whom did not have the same childhood experiences Jesus had had, and they had never seen the famous, holy structure that had shaped their identity, even from afar. The account of events in John's Gospel includes Jesus' use of a "whip of cords" (John 2:15), and in all four Gospels, he overturns the tables of the moneychangers, whose job was to change Roman coins for Hebrew shekels so that Temple-goers could purchase animals for sacrifices.

A common misunderstanding here is that Jesus was upset about the money-changing *per se*. He famously reiterated the Temple's role as the place where God dwelled among his people—"a house of prayer; but you make it a den of robbers" (Matt. 21:13; Luke 19:45). But what robbery was going on in the Temple? Exchanging Roman coins for shekels was a standard part of the Temple system. Instead, what seemed to anger Jesus here most was *where* the moneychangers were working. Many scholars believe that when Jesus cleansed the Temple, his concern was that the transactions for sacrifices were being conducted in the Court of the Gentiles—the place where non-Jews were allowed to participate (in part) in Israelite religion.

In Mark's Gospel alone do we find the key word, derived from the prophet Isaiah, that indicates the Temple's purpose, Jesus' problem with what he sees, and our own identity as Catholics who now find ourselves inheritors of ancient Israelite worship: "My house shall be called a house of prayer for all the *nations*" (11:17; see also Isa. 56:7). "The nations" means Gentiles, non-Jews—most people on the planet earth in the past, present, and future. The Temple therefore turns out to be far bigger than the hundreds of cubits in size it had achieved at the time of Jesus. It was not just a special building representing a special institution, but something pointing beyond all man-made structures and ethnic customs.

It is no surprise, therefore, that Jesus "spoke of the temple of his body" (John 2:21) and shocked the Pharisees by saying that "something greater than the temple is here" (Matt. 12:6). Jesus got upset with his kinsmen who misunderstood Israel's identity and purpose. He says in Matthew's Gospel, "Do not presume to say to yourselves, 'We have Abraham as our father'; for I tell you, God is able from these stones to raise up children to Abraham" (3:9).

In the end, however, Jesus did not dismiss Abraham's sons and daughters, even though some of them dismissed him. Indeed, by founding the Church and entrusting it to St. Peter and the apostles, Jesus was not founding a new school, college, or seminary—let alone a new Temple—but was instead fulfilling God's promise to save the world through one chosen people. Judaism was a people, not an institution, and so would be the Catholic Church that continued from Israel.

Unfortunately, there is still a tendency to think of the faith of Israel as rooted mostly in ethnicity, but Catholics should know better. After all, to this day, our bishops' headwear is hard to distinguish from the yarmulke—and not totally by accident! In the words of Pope Pius XI, all Christians are "Semites spiritually."

Faith as New Life

Two stories from the Gospels that feature non-Jews who believe in Jesus may help illustrate the point that the Catholic

Church is not just buildings, programs, and personnel for some people and not others. Rather, the Catholic Church is where one becomes part of and grows into an all-encompassing life of faithfulness.

The first is the story of the centurion, depicted in Matthew 8:5-13 and Luke 7:1-10. The centurion is not a Jew, and he understands that he has no inherent right to receive the ministry of Israel's Messiah. He is not circumcised, was not raised in the synagogue, and does not keep kosher—he has been formed by completely different institutions from those of the people among whom he lives. Yet he approaches anyway, asking Jesus to heal his paralyzed servant. Jesus agrees to do so, to break Jewish custom by entering the home of a Gentile, and a Roman official to boot.

The centurion issues a statement of humility that Catholics now say in a slightly modified version every time we attend Mass: "Lord, I am not worthy to have you come under my roof; but only say the word, and my servant will be healed" (Matt. 8:8). The centurion is clearly not looking to trade his Roman credentials for Jewish ones; rather, he sees all of his human loyalties subsumed under the vision of reality standing before him. Jesus thus replies, "Truly, I say to you, not even in Israel have I found such faith" (v. 10b). And faith is a divine virtue, given by God to those for whom his service is the highest good.

The second story is that of the Canaanite woman in Matthew 15 (called the Syrophoenician woman in Mark 7:24-30). The first important point is that in the Old Testament, the term *Canaanite* refers to a number of different, historic enemies of Israel. They are the various groups inhabiting the promised land when the Israelites return from Egypt determined to live where God has sent them. For someone belonging broadly to this group to ask for something from Jesus would be even more extraordinary than for a Roman military man to do so. For a woman to do so would be doubly odd.

Jesus ignores the Canaanite woman's initial cries to help her demon-possessed daughter. But she persists, aware that Jesus is not a brand representative for a variety of Judaism. Jesus finally levels with her in a way that seems shocking to us who are used to a false caricature of a Jesus who is "nice" rather than just and righteous. He tells her that he was "sent only to the lost sheep of the house of Israel" (Matt. 15:24), and then he seems to insult her: "It is not fair to take the children's bread and throw it to the dogs" (v. 26).

The Canaanite woman remains undeterred. Like the centurion, she approaches Jesus with an understanding that he is the "Son of David" (v. 22), and that what she desires from him is not properly owed to her. She says to Jesus, "Even the dogs eat the crumbs that fall from their masters' table" (v. 27).

What does Jesus mean by this seeming epithet?

Jesus is not playing the part of gatekeeper for a venerable old institution called Judaism. Rather, his words reveal the opposite intention: precisely because his wider mission is not to Israel *alone*, it must start with Israel and expand. If Jesus had gone around healing anybody and everybody, or if he had denied the importance of his identity as an Israelite, what followed his resurrection and ascension would have been akin to abolishing one institution to start another—out with Judaism, in with Christianity. But Jesus meant to do no such thing. Rather, Jesus made exceptions and expanded his ministry outside Israel as a way to show that what followed would be an expansion on earth of a heavenly reality. We call this reality the kingdom.

Kingdom Language

In my experience, church mission statements are usually more trouble than they are worth. What is it that *our* parish does that the one next door does not? Well, a lot of things . . . and nothing. We may be good at outreach, and our neighbors do beautiful liturgy, but we ought to do better liturgy, and they ought to try a bit harder help people who don't show up on Sundays. At the same time, every community has a particular character—a charism, even—and it is worth identifying and developing.

I am agnostic on the question of getting a committee together to craft a fifty-word blurb for the cover of the bulletin. But if a parish does choose to craft and publish a mission statement, the main thing I would counsel is to be careful how it uses the word *kingdom*, particularly in relation to any version of another word: *build*.

Talk of *building the kingdom* has become common among Catholics and Protestants alike, and for the most part, it is well-meaning. No less an authority than Pope St. John Paul II said in a general audience in 2000,

> All the just of the earth, including those who do not know Christ and his Church, who, under the influence of grace, seek God with a sincere heart (see *Lumen Gentium* 16), are called to build the kingdom of God by working with the Lord, who is its first and decisive builder.[40]

Even with non-Catholics, Catholics build. We seek to make the experience of life in the world more fruitful for others, and institutions like schools, soup kitchens, community centers, service organizations, social clubs, and devotional societies are part of this divine construction project.

There is a danger, however, that some Christians will mistake social service for the heart of the gospel of Jesus Christ. Such thinking mistakes the Church as an institution, where grace happens to be available. In this way, the Mass and, by extension, all Catholic liturgy and ritual become utilitarian—at best, the Lord's body is a pill that infuses our souls with strength to go out somewhere else and make a difference. In the same way, to some people, education is mostly utilitarian, valuable since the contents that we learn may be applied for our own or others' material gain.

Institutions tend to have utopian or at least progressive ends, even where the institution may have a stated conservative viewpoint. That is, every institution works to create more of something, do more of something, expand its reach, and heighten its influence. The Church's institutions unabashedly seek these kinds of ends, but the Church itself is not becoming anything else, going anywhere else, or waiting for us to fix it or finish it. The Catholic Church *is* because Christ *is*. The kingdom of heaven has already come near, and our participation in the liturgy of the Catholic Church is our experience of the veil separating heaven and earth dropping in our midst.

The Catholic Church is not a theory waiting to be put into practice. Nor is its earthly form a mere shadow of a heavenly reality that is to come. It exists. It is a concrete reality, composed of everyone baptized in the name of the Father, and of the Son, and of the Holy Spirit. It is a people, just as God's chosen people Israel were and are a people.

Not an institution. Not a box.

Church and State

The Catholic Church is in quite a bad position today in relation to State and society, masking its true identity and destiny and leaving even its most devoted members at a loss for how to proceed with evangelism.

In the earliest days of the Church, the Jews in Jerusalem who believed that Jesus was their promised Messiah differentiated themselves from other Jews who did not share their view. Although they continued to attend the Temple, eventually, they faced persecution from their kinsmen, as Jesus had foretold in the Gospel according to St. John. In the next few centuries, as the missionary endeavors of Peter, Paul, James, and the rest of the apostolic band spread the Faith throughout the Roman Empire, persecution flared up here and there. But in both directions—toward Judaism and paganism—the Christians knew what they were about. They were a people made up of many peoples, dwelling among many peoples.

As the Church took root in Europe and Christendom was born, being Catholic defined the identity of peoples not as a rebellion, but as a culture—indeed, as civilization. It was obvious to all that the Catholic Church was not an institution, but the wellspring of the moral life of individuals and families and the ground upon which tribes and kingdoms and ultimately modern nation states stood. In a time and place where everyone was baptized (or *almost* everyone—more anon), there was implicit pressure to create laws, maintain norms, and in every conceivable way organize life around the sacramental life of the Catholic Church, whose cathedrals, monasteries, abbeys, and churches were not accidentally the centerpiece of every city, town, and village. That is, the ubiquity of Church institutions and their power to form individuals signaled the identity of the Church as the transcendent marker of identity that defined the group. Even where—or especially where—individuals were *not* personally on fire for the gospel, only the mentally deranged or deficient thought society ought to conform to their dissenting view. The assertion of rights within a theoretical religiously neutral space was simply anachronistic.

In recent centuries in the once thoroughly Catholic societies of the West, however, Christianity has fragmented into groups, which we explored earlier, making its various expressions look more like institutions among others in a broadly

Christian but officially neutral society. For a long time in countries like the United States and France, secularism still maintained an essentially Christian character. Hence, my own parents remember saying the Lord's Prayer in their public schools, and no one—including Jews and other religious minorities—objected on the grounds that some fundamental principle of a separation of Church and State was being violated. In this example, the school was obviously the institution, whereas churches were understood to be something more like the guardians and promoters of the values that everyone agreed ought to underpin all institutions.

In the 1960s, however, things began to change. God was banished to the private sphere, and Christian secularism transformed into a non-religious or even anti-religious version of secularism. In Europe and North America, the Catholic Church, along with Protestant communities, came to dwell in a no man's land between where ancient Christians died for the Faith and the everyday Christian reality where medieval and early modern people lived for the Faith. Being an authentic Catholic had always been a choice, but in the late twentieth century, it became *only* a choice.

As I've noted, the Catholic Church had always had a lot of institutions, but nowadays, it is considered *only* an institution, even if a holy one.

Old World, New World

As a Western man, I believe it is no accident that the seat of the Catholic Church is in Europe. Indeed, Western civilization and the Catholic Church go hand in hand.

Although the Faith has spread to the ends of the earth and, in some cases, is much more vibrant in far-flung places than in the Old World, it is folly to abandon the idea of a Western Christian society. Rather, it is the *Roman*—i.e. Western,

Catholic faith that has transformed many different cultures on other continents. Happily, some of these cultures are now able to reinvigorate the West with the same message that the West once brought to them.

Perhaps the most important part of the witness back to the secular West from African and Asian nations, in particular, is the martyrdom that Catholics and other Christians experience in a context where Church institutions are embattled, if they exist at all. For the most part, persecution and martyrdom happen either in non-Christian authoritarian states that deem any religion a threat (China and North Korea, for example) or from Islamist groups and governments whose totalizing vision of religion excludes the gospel of Jesus Christ.

A Catholic group called Aid to the Church in Need reported that in 2021 and the first part of 2022, 5,000 Christians were killed in various attacks for their faith.[41] In the year 2018, ninety percent of Christians killed for their faith worldwide were Nigerian, and most of them were killed by the Islamist group Boko Haram, according to Ray Cavanagh in an article for *Catholic World Report*.[42] Nonetheless, or perhaps as a result, there are now almost thirty-two million baptized Catholics in Nigeria, representing fifteen percent of the population, as reported by *The Pillar*.[43] The bloody testimony of Catholic Nigerians poses the question to Catholics in the West, where religion is private and institutional: Would we keep it up if there were a decent chance of being killed?

We may soon find out.

A Fighting Faith

Sadly, the still Christ-haunted secular West is experiencing its own attacks, which are certainly smaller in comparison to Nigeria's plight, but all the more shocking because they are taking place not only on soil supposedly claimed for religious toleration but even more significantly in lands where the Catholic Church was once an indisputable way of life. Perhaps the most infamous example in recent years was the murder of the French priest, Fr. Jacques Hamel, in 2016. While celebrating Mass in a church in the northern French city of Rouen, Hamel's throat was cut by terrorists sponsored by the group Islamic State. Four men were convicted of terrorist conspiracy in 2022, and the cause for Hamel's sainthood is now active, with his former church serving as something of a pilgrimage site. France, once known as "the eldest daughter of the Church," is now an officially non-Christian secular country, with a ten percent Muslim population that is not particularly interested in a neutral, religion-free public square.

It seems likely that France, along with the rest of Europe and perhaps even the United States, will continue to see martyrdom in the years to come. Nonetheless, the greatest enemy of the Faith is not the violent designs of other religions' extremists, but rather the indifference of Western society to the truth claims of the Catholic Church. If Catholics thought of their faith as more than a personal choice made possible by institutional structures like churches and schools, they would stand up and mount a challenge to the enemies of Christian culture in the way some medieval and early modern Europeans did.

Although we are coming up short today on figures like Charles Martel and Jan Sobieski, it is still better to chart a course back toward Christian civilization—indeed, toward a Catholic society—instead of either surrendering to a merely personal religion or morbidly anticipating a return to the catacombs. If underground Christianity should become our only option, then so be it. But why go down without a fight, however foolhardy it may seem? People stand up to preserve institutions all the time. How much more sensible is it to insist on the perseverance of a society marked by something much greater than any institution could hope to be?

Ironically, as all institutions fail in the West, the Catholic Church may have an opportunity to reclaim its identity as the ground of communal life, even where communities are smaller and more intentional than a society-wide "people." Just as the ancient Israelites bided their time in Babylon, with a faithful remnant keeping the candle of their God-given identity burning until they could return to a YHWH-centered society, so too should Catholics in the West today hold tight to our once-great cultural heritage in anticipation of its renewal. Catholics who really understand that the Catholic Church is not an institution may help lead the way in the long project of re-establishing a Catholic community that sets the tone for the rest of a nation.

In his prophetic lecture from 1939 called "The Idea of a Christian Society," the Anglican T.S. Eliot described this faithful remnant as "the Community of Christians." He noted that these people would be "composed of both clergy and laity, of the more conscious, more spiritually and intellectually developed of both."[44] Because the Catholic Church is not itself just an institution, the "Community of Christians" can evaluate the Church's institutions for their value among a renewed people of God of a larger scale.

A while back, I mentioned the Cathedral of Notre Dame in Reims, France. I want now to say something about the more famous Notre Dame in Paris.

On April 15, 2019, I had been a Roman Catholic for 109 days, and I was in the thick of unemployment after resigning my ministry in the Episcopal Church. Every day was difficult, but I was spiritually attentive, looking for and expecting God's provision every day. But on that day, I stood at the television set in horror as one of the greatest symbols of Christian civilization went up in flames. The burning of Notre Dame remains all the more heartbreaking—and consonant with the ever-encroaching nihilism of our age—because there is no clear explanation for what happened. It appears not to have been terrorism or malice. It just burned. And although Catholics and non-Catholics worldwide rejoice that the building will be restored more or less to glory, the images of Notre Dame's near demise are illustrative.

On the one hand, obviously the Catholic Church in France—let alone elsewhere on earth—would have endured even if Notre Dame had been reduced to rubble. There would still have been thousands of functioning churches—great ones, small ones, and everything in between. Contrast this fact with what happened to Judaism after the destruction of the Temple a few decades after the life of Christ. Contrast too with what would become of Islam if Mecca disappeared. Christianity is more than any one building or location, however important.

But it is worth considering that the extraordinary beauty and storied history of buildings like Notre Dame point beyond the world to heaven. In other words, we need Notre Dame because it shows us how an entire city and nation once did and could again revolve around a work of human hands that has an otherworldly purpose. Moreover, although few other buildings on earth rival Notre Dame's symbolic value, its existence gives every sacred building—and indeed, every sacred institution rooted in the Catholic Church—something to aspire to. Notre Dame survived the Protestant Reformation and the French Revolution. Today, it still stands amid the official secularism of *la France laïque*, representing the ongoing encounter with the living God who has revealed much more to humanity than an institution.

Sacrament with Institutions

When a person becomes a Catholic, whether baptized as a child or as an adult, he joins the body of Christ as a member of a parish, which is a subtly different thing from a member of a church. Parishes are geographic regions assigned to the pastoral oversight of a bishop, who delegates authority over individual parishes (or sometimes multiple parishes) to his priests. In most cases, the parish church is synonymous with the parish, but, unlike in most Protestant traditions, whether one chooses to go to a local church or prefers an option farther away, that person technically belongs, spiritually, to the physical place where he dwells.

To the untrained eye, the parochial system appears to be about as institutional as anything gets—but in fact, because the parish exists to transform ordinary man into sacramental man, the parish is super-institutional. It is a mark of heavenly citizenship on *terra firma*. Here we may return to our earlier examination of ancient Israel, and how the Catholic Church is both the fulfillment and continuation of God's choice of one chosen nation, one promised land, and one dwelling place on earth in the Temple.

The identity of the Catholic parish is described in the *Catechism of the Catholic Church* in two different places. In paragraph 2179, we read that "a parish is a definite community of the Christian faithful established on a stable basis within a particular church," and "the pastoral care of the parish is entrusted to a pastor as its own shepherd under the authority of the diocesan bishop." If I have not stated it plainly enough throughout this chapter, let me put straight now: the Catholic Church is a people, a people in a place, and a people in every place. But there is one more all-important element, and the *Catechism* describes it in paragraph 2226: "The parish is the eucharistic community and the heart of the liturgical life of Christian families."

Eucharistic. Community.

Although there are precisely seven sacraments of the Church, the Church itself has the essential character of an overarching sacrament. It is where the body of Christ receives the body of Christ—where Christ, who is "all in all," dwells where I am, and also where Christ is present in full to a brother Christian in a faraway parish in a faraway land. As Jesus says, "I tell you, something greater than the Temple is here" (Matt. 12:6). What we have here, then, is not just one super-institutional focal point for a relatively small nation of God's people. Nor do we have in the Church merely an institution with a universal spirit of inquiry shared among people in different cities and countries. Rather, the Catholic Church is the experience of the common destiny of man—eucharistic man—transformed into Christ by Christ, living in a present that intersects with eternity. In every parish, in every home, in every institution, and in every heart, Jesus is Lord.

CHAPTER 5

The Club Box

At the beginning of the film *Annie Hall*, Woody Allen makes a self-effacing remark, which he attributes to Groucho Marx: "I never want to belong to any club that would have someone like me for a member." I have never shared Woody's view. On the contrary—and forgive me my pride—I have tended to look askance at most clubs, groups, organizations, and gatherings and wonder what they could possibly offer me. If I am going to belong to something, it had better be good.

To wit, I have had some difficulty over the years choosing where, how, and how long to belong to things. Being with a group once or twice may be all right, but do I want to be there every month or week or, God forbid, every day? I do, however, have in my mind a Platonic ideal of a club that caters to my whims, is happy to have me when I want to belong, but makes no demands on me when I would rather go my own way. As an intellectual and a gourmand, this club I have in mind looks an awful lot like the real gentleman's clubs that exist to this day along Pall Mall in London, although they are lamentably less rambunctious now than they were once portrayed in the stories of P.G. Wodehouse.

Even a fine fellows' establishment in London, however, leaves me wanting in the end (not that I would ignore the

81

opportunity to take a place at the Athenaeum or the Carlton if offered). On one recent occasion, where I spent an evening in one of these clubs, I could not help but think, as a married man and a father, that no club could ever provide the conviviality of the family dinner table in my modest suburban American bungalow. Likewise, my gracious host lamented that there were various ongoing disputes among the club members about replacing carpets, the prices of food, and various other quasi-domestic matters, which, again, reminded me that I had plenty of that sort of thing at home already. I *think* my wife and children, if put to a vote, would keep me in the leadership position of our little domestic organization, and I take my duties seriously there. In a sense, I have chosen to belong there; but more often than not I have the Talking Heads' lyrics running through my head: "How did I get here?"

By God's mysterious grace, belonging is more like a gift I have received than an option I have selected.

As a Christian, I am glad that in reality, the Church is no more a club than my family is, although, unlike my family, the Church surely does have entrance requirements. Nonetheless, churches—large ecclesial groups and individual congregations—sometimes function as if they were primarily clubs that have a particular flavor of Christianity as an organizing principle. By this logic, a country club is for golf, and a church is for worship, and the buildings and membership groups take on a certain character of belonging. If we unboxed a particular parish, for example, it would have a certain "club" feel to it. We could see what kind of person spends Sundays with the Presbyterians versus the Pentecostals. It would be interesting to note how a Catholic Church in an Italian-American neighborhood differed from an Irish-American neighborhood. And am I the only one who finds the term "black churches" or "the Black Church" a little unusual for a group whose larger membership consists of every race under the sun?

Where to Be?

In the spring of 2018, I was in agony about belonging.

I was an Episcopal priest then, and I fit in pretty well with my "club," although I was not of the manor born. Rather, from the vantage point of my co-religionists, I had made it professionally, and by my own choice. There were lots of other ways to be a Christian and serve in ministry, after all. And in fact, in order to become an Episcopal priest, I had had to pass through several committees over a number of years—kind of a membership process, really, and it was not at all clear to me along the way that I would get through.

(In retrospect, I ask myself, why did I subject myself to such scrutiny? Why did I want to be *there* so badly? God only knows.)

Anyway, I made it. And while serving for more than six years at a wonderful Episcopal parish in Florida, I had begun to make a name for myself as a capable leader among a small band of conservatives in the increasingly liberal Anglican Communion. At the relatively young age of thirty-seven, I had been invited by the Episcopal bishop of Tennessee, based in Nashville, to join him as his canon to the ordinary, the equivalent of a vicar general in a Catholic diocese. With this position came a respectable middle-class salary and even a signing bonus, allowing me to buy my first home for my family. We settled nicely in Nashville, and we quickly built a community of church colleagues, neighbors, and school friends.

But all the while, I was struggling with whether I could remain an Anglican or would ultimately have to become Catholic. The perks of my new position had made me temporarily forgetful of my crisis, but upon assuming the role, I was suddenly in the uncomfortable position of being a brand representative.

In my experience, one cannot be an effective right hand to the king if he is not sure the leadership he is exercising should even be happening. On the controversial issues of the day, no one seemed to care if I was personally conservative on questions of sexuality, for example. It did not much matter to our clergy and people that we had different opinions about divestment from Israel or reparations for slavery or carbon neutrality or any number of issues *du jour*. Since our ecclesial group had basically decided those matters already—and in a secular progressive direction to boot—my personal opinion had very little to do with the job I was given.

My ecclesial group had no use for a doctrinaire canary in its coal mine, even if such a creature could have still been of any use (alas, the ship had long sailed). It suddenly hit me that if I was in the club, which was an apt metaphor for the Episcopal Church for many reasons, then my choice was either to enjoy its material benefits or else resign and find somewhere else to belong. As at the beginning of my Anglican journey, everyone still agreed at this later stage that there was always somewhere else to go. Why force yourself as a square peg into a round hole?

For a while, I tried to get on with things, accepting my duties at "the club" helping my bishop administer a large budget, making clergy appointments, overseeing diocesan staff, and attending all manner of church meetings all over middle Tennessee and beyond. One of those meetings took place in early May of 2018.

Long, Strange Trip

As part of my responsibilities to my bishop, I was asked to attend a meeting of my fellow first lieutenants from Episcopal dioceses from all over the southeast United States. On this occasion, the gathering was to be held in Greenville, South Carolina, and since I had a family member I wanted to visit in nearby Asheville, North Carolina, I decided to make the drive east through the gorgeous Great Smoky Mountains. I had been thinking a lot about my future—whether I could keep up the façade of enjoying a modicum of ecclesiastical privilege that afforded my family a comfortable American lifestyle, or whether I would have to face my wife with the news that I felt compelled to surrender to the Catholic Church. I thought the drive could help clear my head, and my companion on the way was the audiobook of George Weigel's biography of Pope St. John Paul II, *Witness to Hope*.

Hour after hour of my drive from Nashville to Greenville, I was drawn deeper into the life of this great modern saint, and into the reality of the Catholic Church. Over and over again the courageous words of Karol Józef Wojtyła rang in my ears: "Be not afraid."

It may sound a little funny to cradle Catholics, but of all the things I was afraid of, blowing up my life and putting my family into financial uncertainty were not at the top of the list. Most of all I wondered, would I feel as if I belonged? Would someone whose spiritual bloodline was Protestant in all four directions be able to fit in somewhere else? As a Protestant—even as a High Church Anglican—I had a particular culture that I would have to leave behind. Even if I believed everything the Catholic Church taught, would I be able to live comfortably within it?

A word of clarity on this matter came at the end of my trip.

While on a break from meeting with my Episcopalian colleagues, I sent a message to a friend, a married Catholic priest who had formerly been an Episcopal priest. As it happened, my friend had lived in Greenville when he converted, and he fired me back a message right away: Do not leave the area without visiting Fr. Jay Scott Newman. Following my friend's command, I called Fr. Newman, pastor at St. Mary's Catholic Church in historic downtown Greenville, and he invited me to his office on my way out of town.

When I met Fr. Newman, I was immediately struck both by his warmth and his earnestness. He is a large, serious man, whose kindness shines through immediately. He asked me to call him Scott (a professional courtesy for a fellow clergyman, perhaps, but one that strongly increased my sense of belonging). He then led me into his office, where I noticed two portraits flanking his sitting area—one of John Henry Newman, and the other of John Paul II. I pointed out his obvious connection to Newman's name, and we spoke for a while about the Victorian churchman's influence on both of us. Although I was a lifelong Christian and Scott came from an atheist background, we had both spent time as different varieties of Protestants, and ultimately as Anglicans, before facing the dilemma of whether to enter full communion with Rome. I then remarked on the portrait of John Paul II and how Weigel's biography had moved me on my drive through the Smokies. Fr. Newman, in his humble, gentlemanly way, casually remarked that Weigel was his close friend, and that *Witness to Hope* was completed right there at St. Mary's, where Weigel would sometimes come on retreat to write.

The coincidences were piling up all over the place.

As I was about to leave, I confided to Fr. Newman that I worried I might not fit in the Catholic Church. Would I just be exchanging one set of problems for another? As we stood up, he looked me square in the eyes and told me perhaps the most important thing anyone said to me in my entire life as a Christian: "Andrew, the Catholic Church is perfectly awful. But it's the real deal."

With those words, it was game, set, and match. I was not swapping membership cards from one club to another. I was moving beyond all this club business once and for all.

Bygone Club Days

As longtime Catholics know from the Church's history of wrangling, compromise, and sometimes bitterness with regard to liturgical changes, it is rare to find a Catholic who believes he gets everything he wants out of worship. Many former Protestants I know regret that their social life as Catholics demands less of them but also offers less to them than what they had known in their previous traditions. Some Catholics struggle to find a way to connect to a parish community apart from dashing in and out of a fifty-eight-minute Mass in a cavernous modern building.

But the problem with belonging is even bigger. Whereas in the United States, most people once belonged not only to churches and to groups within churches, but to an array of civic and educational organizations, too, these days, we are less connected and more isolated. If, therefore, a person chooses to join any church today, it is likely he wishes there were a club-like element to it. And for older churchgoers who remember a civilization whose organizations have almost all disintegrated (see the previous chapter), they may emphasize the identity of their church as something like a club because it is the closest thing to the way things used to be.

But if the Catholic Church *were* a club, it would be a pretty bad one to join. Fr. Newman said as much in his parting words to me. The most obvious reason in recent years to stay away from the Catholic Church is the clerical sex abuse scandals that began coming to light in the early 2000s. I have a few friends, also former Episcopalian ministers like me, whose spiritual directors prescribed for them to read revolting Grand Jury reports chronicling decades of crimes against young people at the hands of priests. My friends were rightly disturbed, but not deterred from their course of finally coming into full communion with the Catholic Church. Like me, they made their peace with the fact that the Catholic Church is not a club with an impressive history marred by an embarrassing recent batch of ejected members. Again, perfectly awful and the real deal.

My friends' experience aside, the horrific behavior of clerics has driven some Catholics out of the Church, kept otherwise willing seekers from taking the final step in, and made the task of Catholic evangelism more difficult for those of us who remain. But also, Catholics and non-Catholics alike often do not realize how scandals at the heart of one of the biggest organizations on earth—and particularly one with the holiest of aspirations—have helped undermine society's overall trust in organizations *per se*. In other words, declining membership in the Catholic Church is not just another symptom of a culture less interested in God, or of belonging to groups with their neighbors. Rather, it is reasonable to approach the situation from the other way around. With an already false perception of Catholicism as a particularly lofty club, followed by the revelation of this club's inadequacies, the desire to belong to *anything* may decrease.

The film *Spotlight* depicts the work of *Boston Globe* journalists whose reporting in 2002 was the first wave in what proved to be an ongoing typhoon. Another film of the same period, however, speaks more subtly and more profoundly about the effects of clerical abuse. Martin Scorsese's dark 2006 gangster movie *The Departed* is a look at what happens when the devil fills space that should be occupied by the spirit of Christ and his saints. Loosely based on the life of real-life Boston mafia boss Whitey Bulger, *The Departed* demonstrates the connection between the cancer of wicked behavior among clergy and a culture of mayhem that spreads out from the festering wounds of abuse. It is strongly implied that the crooked cop, played by Matt Damon, was sexually abused by a priest, and Jack Nicholson's character, Frank Costello, becomes a sinister paternal stand-in. Costello declares: "I don't want to be a product of my environment. I want my environment to be a product of me. Years ago we had the Church. That was only a way of saying—we had each other."

Survey Says . . .

In September 2023, the Pew Research Center reported that only 15 percent of Americans say they trust the government to do the right thing "just about always," compared to 75 percent in 1958.[45] Political leaders have tended to settle for mediocrity in an age when heroic sacrifice is no longer required of them or anyone else. Many religious leaders are mediocre, too, or worse. Whereas Christianity long played a role in society as a unifying force that prescribed common goals and a common destination, in recent times, Christian communities have largely lost their nerve, and they have instead begun affirming spiritual journeys but neglecting or even rejecting immutable spiritual ideals.

The Christian tradition of pilgrimage teaches us that much is learned along the way, but we all know that a journey without a destination is pointless. For a time in the twentieth century—well before peak churchgoing after World War II—some Christians did an admirable job engaging with the narrative of a meaningful journey amid a wasteland of personal options. And no one Christianized the modernist cycle of man's search for meaning better than T.S. Eliot, whom I mentioned in the previous chapter, in his set of poems called *The Four Quartets*.

The problem is that most people didn't and don't read or
know anything about the high modernism of a Christian like
Eliot. By the 1950s, a relativist worldview had begun eroding
the foundations of once-Christian societies. Yet the longing
for solid ground remained. The existence of a true spiritual
home became a myth—but a myth that continued to fire the
imagination of individuals and society.

Take the example of the famous Beat Generation writer
Jack Kerouac. In 1957, Kerouac published his *roman à clef*, a
book called *On the Road*, a barely fictional countercultural
travelogue, which he called "a story about two Catholic bud-
dies roaming the country in search of God." In the book, the
characters Sal Paradise and Dean Moriarty (based on Kerouac's
friend Neal Cassady) act out their longing to belong—not to
the Masonic lodges or bowling leagues or even churches of
their peers, but to *the real* itself, which the Catholic Church
should, but often does not, articulate well enough. Like many
of his age and ours, Kerouac tried more than his share of illicit
and artificial replacements for this ultimate fulfillment. Not
surprisingly, Kerouac found all these imitations of true fulfillment lacking in substance. The mass-marketed consumer
goods pushed by the advertising industry, fictionalized in the
television show *Mad Men*, did no better than booze or sex.

More recently, in 1992, a young idealist named Christopher
McCandless went on his own quest for ultimate meaning and
ended up dying in the Alaskan wilderness. His story is told
in Jon Krakauer's best-selling book *Into the Wild*, which was
made into a Hollywood movie in 2007 by director Sean Penn.
McCandless, played by Emile Hirsch, graduates from an elite
college, gives away his money to charity, and drops off the
grid in a late twentieth-century imitation of Henry David
Thoreau, the nineteenth-century intellectual godfather to the
aimlessness of our own day. But whereas Thoreau's retreat

to the woods still meant a warm fire and a comfortable bed at night, McCandless, near starvation and alone, was driven by desperate hunger to eat poisonous berries that he knew would kill him.

We eventually learn that McCandless was abused by his father as a child, and he rejected his parents' religion and the Church. He was nonetheless desperate for truth—the safe home with a God and a Church that he could not even imagine and thus that he tried to construct for himself. His predicament is all too common. He says in the film, "God's place is all around us; it is in everything and in anything we can experience. People just need to change the way they look at things." But in assuming that God is everywhere, Christopher McCandless failed to find him anywhere specific. The familiar failure of this kind of spiritual quest by all age groups in our world today is epitomized tragically in the film when McCandless literally dies homeless. His club of one proved inadequate.

As a child of divorced parents, but also as a natural melancholic and intellectual, I myself have sought the places of authenticity and belonging that Jack Kerouac and Christopher McCandless were searching for in their respective ways. I cringe now at the thought of my solitary freshman year of college, for example. Like so many young people away at school, I reached a point after Christmas break when I was not sure I was going to be able to hack it. It was the spring of 1999, and I walked up and down a hill every day to classes on my urban campus, and I retreated to my room each evening to watch a trusty rotating set of movies and listen to familiar favorite albums to keep my soul from tipping into despair. I went into churches but never stayed. I looked into an Evangelical ministry meeting once but decided not to go in. I wanted God, and I wanted to belong, but nothing felt right.

Then one afternoon after class, I flipped on the TV and learned that two young men had shot up their teachers and classmates at Columbine High School in Colorado.

For people now tragically used to mass shootings, it can hardly be overstated how shocking the Columbine massacre was then. I was especially devastated because I had just graduated from high school a few months earlier, and my large public high school in Florida was an awful lot like Columbine. I imagined that the massacre could have happened to me and my friends. But actually, in the hidden depths of my heart, I asked myself whether, if certain things had gone just a little bit differently in my life, I might have ended up like the disturbed young men who, no doubt under the influence of the demonic, took out their youthful delusions of persecution on other kids and teachers. As a nineteen-year-old college freshman, I knew I was a little lost. But when Columbine happened, it startled me to think what it would take for my life to go off track.

That summer, I went to Paris on a study abroad course. I made new friends, improved my French, and visited every church and museum in the city. Being on the road—fully alive and sharing joy with others—was wonderful therapy. I had found my people, and my journey suddenly felt as though it was back on track. But the goal of my life was still not very clear. The situation is the same for so many people, young and old, today.

Dystopia: Just Say No

In Cormac McCarthy's devastating 2006 novel *The Road*, we find a setting that has become increasingly common in Western fiction: the post-apocalyptic quest for safety and community. Steven King's 1978 novel *The Stand* was a pioneering work in this genre. George Miller's *Mad Max* films from the same era point forward to later efforts like Danny Boyle's *28 Days Later*, Terry Gilliam's *Twelve Monkeys*, and Alfonso Cuarón's *Children of Men*. Just after the turn of the new millennium, prestige television took up the mantle of apocalyptic storytelling in shows like *Lost*, *The Walking Dead*, and *Last Man on Earth*. But McCarthy's novel, also made into a film, is a particularly valuable specimen to examine how our need for spiritual belonging far exceeds what any club could provide.

The Road is a sparse, devastating study of a man and his son, wandering ashen roads in constant fear of robbers and cannibals in the long aftermath of an unexplained cataclysm. Neither the man nor the boy is ever named, and we learn in passing that a wife and mother was once with them, but she took her own life in despair. Even a few pages of the McCarthy's bleak description of the desperate attempt to stay alive leads the most contented reader to ask himself from time to time, "Why bother?" But like great survival novels, going all the way back to Daniel Defoe's great *Robinson Crusoe*, *The Road* is a reminder that all lives are salvage operations.

There is a scene near the end of *The Road* where the man boards a rusted ocean liner, looking for food and supplies, clearly calling to mind Crusoe's attempt to save what he can from his wrecked ship. The point is, the road is hard no matter what. The pitiless gray skies and constant threat of danger and starvation in *The Road* are merely extreme forms of our own condition on earth. To get through it, everyone needs faith, which is "the substance of things hoped for, the conviction of things not seen" (Heb. 11:1).

The man in McCarthy's novel often reminds his son, who has never known a life other than post-catastrophic wandering, to "carry the fire." Jesus tells us, "You are the light of the world" (Matt. 5:14). At one point, the boy is overwhelmed with sadness, thinking of his lonely future, and asks, "Is it real? The fire?" His father replies, "Yes it is," leading to the inevitable follow-up from a kid: "Where is it? I don't know where it is." His father tells him, with the same mysterious reassurance of Christ proclaiming the nearness of the kingdom of heaven, "Yes you do. It's inside you. It was always there. I can see it."[46] In another scene, the man looks "along the interstate" through "long lines of charred and rusting cars" and sees his son on the desolate road "looking back at him from some unimaginable future, glowing in that waste like a tabernacle."[47]

Counterculture for the Culture

Maybe Woody Allen's comment about not wanting to belong to a club that would have someone like him as a member is not as ironical or even silly as it may first appear. Because the Catholic Church is not a club, and because it proposes itself as the ultimate reality, every one of its members ought to feel slightly ill at ease or even unworthy to belong. Just as St. Peter asks Jesus, "To whom shall we go?" Catholics are in the holy dilemma of belonging to something that offers no alternatives. Everyone is called to belong, and therefore no one entirely gets what he wants. The questions someone exploring Catholicism might ask himself, therefore, are not far from Allen's: How could I possibly take my place in something perfectly holy when I am flawed? How can God leave it to me to choose him?

The answer from the Church and its members is, again, asserting itself as something different from human categories of belonging. We are, in a way, the anti-club—just as, in a way, most clubs have a tendency to become anti-Christ. And I mean here "anti" in the sense of "in place of"—even churches, when they function more like clubs than the mystical body of Christ, are an alternative to rather than an instantiation of the Catholic Church. In this way, we conclude by considering again the Church's identity as a countercultural culture-maker: God so loved the world that he sent his son to transform it.

Clubs are places of conformity—but in many respects, clubs actually exist to prescribe and uphold a conformity to ideals that may not be present in the wider culture. I mentioned before the famed gentlemen's clubs on Pall Mall in London. To my knowledge, these are all still places that require neckties, forbid talking on cell phones in certain areas, and even favor certain conversation topics over others. When I met my magazine editor friend at his club, he took me to a special set of chairs, which was the only place in the building where men were permitted to "talk shop." In this way, my friend's club was insisting upon an order within itself that it wished to see its members promote to a wider world that has little regard for such things. Less noticeably, other clubs or dues-paying organizations committed to certain causes exist precisely because the members wish to work among themselves for the improvement or change related to matters *outside*.

The Catholic Church, at its best, functions in such a way that its members grow and change, making the world outside its walls a different, better place, too. The Church's rich tradition of Catholic social teaching, for example, ensures that all Catholics subsume their class and partisan commitments beneath gospel basics that fill up all the niches in the woodwork of ethical behavior. To belong to the Catholic Church, then, is to take seriously *all* matters that require both a particular kind of personal comportment among fellow members and a general bearing and commitment to action for the sake of others in the world. Neither Jack Kerouac's nor Christopher McCandless's desire for belonging apart from the corruption of society is quite what membership in the anti-club of the Catholic Church offers, but both are more or less on the right track.

Simply put, the anti-club of the Catholic Church invites everyone to become a member and find total comfort in belonging, but it also requires every member to be transformed for the sake of being better participants in the world outside. The best human clubs may aspire to similar ideals, but none is capable of achieving them. Most clubs don't even have pretensions of any such thing. Rather, quite understandably, they are affinity groups for certain people (and not others) who want to be a certain way (and not most other ways), who perhaps prefer a shoe unboxing video to a cosmetics one. The Catholic Church is something else.

CHAPTER 6

The Escape Box

There are few more distressing tales than the stories of runaways. With the world so cruel and difficult to navigate, it takes an abysmal situation to prompt a person to choose complete uncertainty over somewhere to lay his head. Nonetheless, we can all imagine a situation where we would be willing to take our chances on the street rather than endure a home environment where our life or our dignity is in jeopardy.

Occasionally, a sad runaway saga has a happy ending. Someone is adopted into a loving family or welcomed into a safe community. In such happy circumstances, however, more hurt may result from idealizing the new place as perfect and problem-free. Even a good home can be a messy place.

Conversely, the sad version of the story is one of total loss and death, where someone flees an old hell for a new one. In this case, because someone knows homes only as broken places, that person is unfortunately drawn from one bad abode to the next. Just as heartbreaking are cases where a person is so traumatized by his home life or family of origin that he rejects the whole idea of belonging. These decisions to escape to nowhere seem to go against the basic human instinct for belonging.

Why?

Our fundamental stories as humans center on the reality and necessity of home and our journey to find it: running toward belonging rather than fleeing danger. And if the Church is meant to be our truest home on earth, then we must get right about what this home may and may not offer. What we would not find if we unboxed the Church is merely an escape for runaways from other ecclesial traditions, let alone from the evils of the world.

Tales of Homecoming

Most of the great stories from every age and place in human history are about homecoming. In the Book of Genesis, God tells Abram, "Go from your country and your kindred and your father's house to the land that I will show you" (12:1). The great nation born in this new home is called back again in the book of Exodus after 400 years of slavery, and the books of Leviticus, Numbers, and Deuteronomy are all about wandering homeward. In the Greek tradition, Homer's *Odyssey* is the story of a man coming home from the Trojan War. In Latin, Virgil's *Aeneid* picks up after the Trojan War, this time inventing a hero's journey toward the foundation of the Roman homeland.

Fast-forwarding a few thousand years, most of us know the memorable tag line from *The Wizard of Oz,* "there's no place like home." *The Hobbit* is also called *There and Back Again*, and *The Lord of the Rings* is an even more important journey there and an even longer way back. *Spider-Man: Homecoming* depicts Peter Parker, newly returned from being drafted into the Avengers, settling down to protect his family, friends, and school.

The examples of homecoming in literature are endless, and in most cases, they teach us that home is not a guarantee of safety or even happiness. Home is not somewhere to which we escape; rather, it is where we belong.

The people of ancient Israel not only spend forty years trying to get across the Jordan River, but also spend many decades afterward fighting for the land that God once gave them and promises for them again. Odysseus returns to find his wife and land in the keeping of another man, and he responds violently. Dorothy's family farm is destroyed. Frodo, Sam, Pippin, and Merry return to the Shire to find its trees cut down and its government overthrown by a mad wizard, and so they fight a necessary battle and get to work making things right again. There is no rest for Aeneas or Peter Parker, either. Home is everything, but it is not easy.

No Safe Space

In our increasingly fragmented world, in every culture on earth today, there is a longing for home. It is in the depth of our nature to desire belonging. And the further many people drift from the norm of family, faith, country, and community, the more we find this longing for home placed in unusual places.

Take, for instance, a social eruption that occurred on the campus of Yale University in 2015. A faculty member named Erika Christakis (the wife of Nicholas Christakis, the master of one of Yale's residential colleges) sent an email to students to engage them on the question of culturally sensitive Halloween costumes. She conjured up images from my own trick-or-treat experiences in the 1980s, when we were told our candy might be lethally compromised by razor blades or foreign substances. Only nowadays, the fear lies in dressing in a way that could be interpreted as offensive.[48] Instead of giving in to a need to be protected from offense, Christakis argued, perhaps young people could use challenging situations as an opportunity to become more mature. That is, maybe the juvenile ritual of Halloween could be a reminder to these young Yalies that they came to college to grow up. They are not at home, and their teachers are not their parents—but even if they were at home with their families, what would they do if a sibling dressed some way they disapproved of?

Christakis's email was not well received. Students staged protests and began demanding that she and her husband both be removed from their positions. In a charged confrontation captured on video, one student screamed at Nicholas Christakis, "You were supposed to create a home! This is our home!" The moment epitomized what Greg Lukianoff and Jonathan Haidt had just written in a long article for the *Atlantic* magazine called "The Coddling of the American Mind" (now a book), in which they criticized the "ultimate aim" of making college campuses "safe spaces" that "punish anyone who interferes with that aim, even accidentally."[49]

In another article called "The Yale Problem Begins in High School," Haidt points to a victimhood culture that is particularly prevalent among wealthy, well-educated young people. Their identity is bound not to the hard duty of social cohesion, but to a need to avoid pain—to imagine that "home" is the place to which you escape from reality. Safety and never sacrifice.

People's delusions about society's obligation to them can be annoying if not infuriating. They are also pitiable. After all, selfish sensitivity is simply the water many of us are swimming in. And quite possibly, what appears to be irrational or even hysterical aversion to offense in our culture may be rooted in an understandable desire to belong—to have a home. But there has to be a better way—a real home. The Church has always been just such a home amid the infinite uncertainties of life on earth.

The desire for safe space runs the other way in the culture wars. Take an example from the corporate world. In 2017, an engineer at Google named James Damore responded to a request for feedback from a diversity training he had attended at work. He wrote a memo to his co-workers, calling the company an "ideological echo chamber," which did not include voices with ideas for how to achieve goals such as gender equality in ways that did not conform to the company's progressive ethos. Damore included charts and statistics and tried to be forthright about his own biases so that he could identify the biases of others.

Damore's review was a bit bombastic. However, his motivation appeared to be discontentment with the same misguided allegiance to safety and the construction of an artificial home that we see in the events at Yale two years earlier. Like a college campus on steroids, Google's campus seeks to project an environment where a worker is taken care of in every tangible way. Damore was fired—put out of the house for challenging the family norms. And whether he was right or wrong in his critique of the culture at one of the largest corporations on earth, the point is that he did not feel as though he belonged. He worked for a company that wanted him to feel right at home in the workplace, and he did not.

It makes perfect sense for someone from a broken, dysfunctional, or abusive family of origin to look for a new, safe community to call "home." Ironically, the highest achievers in the United States—the kind of people who go to Yale and work at Google—are also overwhelmingly likely to come from stable families of origin with enough money and an emotionally mature, married mother and father. For many other people in our world, however, life has not always felt safe. Because of sad circumstances and the occasional countercultural choice, plenty of people even in affluent societies today have no fixed homes. There is no safe space for them.

Nowhere to Go

In May 2019, Kevin Fagan of the *San Francisco Chronicle* reported that despite spending $300 million a year, the city of San Francisco saw its homeless population rise in just two years by 17 percent, to a total of more than 8,000 people.[50] In nearby Los Angeles, the problem was even worse. *The Guardian* reported that in the span of one year, the homeless population had increased to "more than 36,000 homeless people in the city of LA, and nearly 59,000 across LA county, a 16 percent and 12 percent uptick respectively."[51] Again, there was no lack of energy or resources thrown at the problem, with more than $600,000 spent in Los Angeles County. Even apart from all the complex economic, sociological, and psychological factors, it remains a no-brainer of Christian charity to help people attain their basic needs of food, clothing, and shelter.

When I was an Anglican clergyman, I spent at least one day a month serving lunch with a group of parishioners to homeless people in downtown Orlando, Florida. I began to see the same faces month after month, and I made friends. I was often asked to pray with and for people, and to provide help beyond the cup of soup and plate of pasta or sandwiches I was helping to hand out. There were often legal aid representatives and job counselors on hand, too. And among all the benefits found inside the four walls of the building, perhaps the most cherished one was air-conditioning, an amenity that only the public library and a few other places they were allowed to go afforded them. For thirty minutes, there was respite from the typical ninety-plus-degree heat and humidity of Central Florida.

In the background of the chaotic environment of this house of nourishment, respite, and empowerment were a couple of large murals. The largest depicted a black man with his arms outstretched at least ten feet in each direction, preparing for an embrace. A large crowd of men and women stood behind him in solidarity. For many people, and especially those who wander in the world without stable roots, friends come to replace kin as family. But whether we come from a great family or an awful one, a new kinship that has nothing to do with deans of student life or the heads of human resources is at the heart of identity as a Christian. Jesus sets the tone:

> "Who is my mother, and who are my brethren?" And stretching out his hand toward his disciples, he said, "Here are my mother and my brethren! For whoever does the will of my Father in heaven is my brother, and sister, and mother" (Matt. 12:48-50).

He intensifies the meaning of the new home and family in Luke's Gospel:

> Truly I say to you, there is no man who has left house or wife or brothers or parents or children, for the sake of the kingdom of God, who will not receive manifold more in this time, and in the age to come eternal life (18:28-30).

The Church is a different kind of home. And coming home to the Church has the shape of the great stories—not an escape, but an arrival. There is no need within the Church for the anxiety over belonging that we see in the artificially constructed safe spaces of Western culture today. A healthy Church, like a healthy family, is a symphony hall, not an echo chamber. The players have to cooperate—and granted, sometimes they're not so good at that—but the building's purpose and their role in it are beyond question.

Something You Don't Deserve

The Giving Tree by Shel Silverstein is one of the most beloved of all children's books. The first time I read it to my kids, I was overwhelmed with emotion. It had been many years since I had last read it—when I was a child myself. I must have identified strongly then with the boy who loved his tree and played on her branches, but as a man in my thirties, I identified much more strongly with the older version of the character, who keeps coming back to his old tree because he has nowhere else to go. "Why are you crying, Daddy?" my daughter asked. "Because this boy is lost," I said spontaneously. I had completely forgotten that the boy asks the tree, "Why don't I have this happiness thing you're telling me about?"

It was devastating. Suddenly I wondered: Where are the boys' parents? What is his home life like? Where is he being formed to be a good man?

Written in 1964, *The Giving Tree* is a prophetic tale of the increasingly isolated postmodern person. I was also moved as I read it for the first time in years because I noticed how the tree loved the boy despite his selfishness. Even broken people and a broken culture should never abandon hope of deep connection and permanent belonging. The boy always took from the tree rather than doing anything to deserve her love, but she gave it anyway. He could have stayed away in shame, but he returned in the end, finally humbled and able only at the bitter end to face reality. That's home.

Robert Frost's poem "The Death of the Hired Man" is a more grown-up expression of a similar theme. At the start of Frost's poem, a woman named Mary warns her husband, Warren, that a former hired hand, Silas, has returned unexpectedly. Silas has proved himself a good worker at times, but untrustworthy. He is now old and has nowhere to go.

He has a rich brother, but he is ashamed to face him. Silas has returned promising to work hard, and Mary assures Warren, "He's changed. Wait till you see." But then she shifts gears, pleading with her husband to care for Silas, who is asleep in front of the stove, because "he has come home to die: You needn't be afraid he'll leave you this time." Warren replies,

> "Home is the place where, when you have to go there,
> They have to take you in."
> "I should have called it
> Something you somehow haven't to deserve."[52]

Is either *The Giving Tree* or "Death of the Hired Man" a tale of escape? No. They are touching, humane meditations on belonging in a world where nothing is safe.

The Prodigal

Jesus' Parable of the Prodigal Son (or the Parable of the Prodigal and His Brother, or the Parable of the Lost Son, or various other titles) is a profound, beloved meditation on homecoming and belonging. It is the most famous of three parables in Luke 15 about loss and gain. The Parable of the Lost Sheep and the Parable of the Lost Coin pave the way for one of the great little stories in all of literature, and it happens to be sacred for Christians, as all of Scripture is.

Not surprisingly, the prodigal son is cited four times in the *Catechism of the Catholic Church* to teach the faithful about various related things: the proclamation of the kingdom of God (545), the forgiveness of sins (2839), entrusting ourselves to our Father in heaven (1700), and the process of conversion and repentance (1439). With the Parable of the Prodigal Son, we also can apply so much of what we have discussed so far about the desire for a true home that is no mere escape.

Many parents can attest to how different two children in the same house can be. Such is the case with the two sons of the father Jesus describes in Luke 15. The older brother is the dutiful one, the one who knows where he belongs from the start and stays put. The younger brother is the wanderer, the *prodigal* (which means "reckless" or "extravagant"). Like the boy in *The Giving Tree*, he takes everything he can get and goes off to do his own thing. But as happens to us all, tough times come to the younger brother, and these times are much tougher when we are detached from our network of support, our home.

As also happens frequently to us, the younger brother's tough times are the result of his own self-indulgence and carelessness. He wants out of his new, reckless life, but it is far from certain that going back to his old one will be a pleasant experience, if it is even possible. He is tortured by the thought that his father's hired hands—people like Robert Frost's subject—are enjoying the benefits of his father's home while he feeds the pigs and starves in a strange land. Completely lost, the prodigal son hopes against hope that home really does mean the place where, when you have to go, they have to take you.

His father does take him, of course—and not merely as an expression of sympathy for a pathetic escapee, but as an act of joy for a beloved son. Jesus tells us, "While he was yet at a distance, his father saw him and had compassion, and ran and embraced him and kissed him" (v. 20). Our heavenly Father greets us as we approach him and his Church as well, with all our brokenness in tow.

When new Christians are made in holy baptism, they are frequently clothed in white garments before eventually coming to the eucharistic feast. Likewise, the prodigal son is put in his father's best robe and given the fatted calf. But the older brother is upset . . . and it is perfectly normal that he is.

There may be occasions where faithful Catholics feel a slight rebuff at the overwhelming greeting they see given to brand-new Christians and former Protestants who have come into communion with the Church. Some Catholics may feel that the Church, led and represented by our spiritual father, the pope, goes out too far to meet the culture rather than asking the culture to come to us. We get used to our home having a particular character. Newcomers and late returners can naturally create a certain tension in an already established dynamic. But the father in Jesus' story invites us all to celebrate as one family. In the economy of God, what is new never takes away from what is old. One person's longstanding virtue is not diminished by another's sudden abandonment of vice. Again in Luke's Gospel, the father explains, "You are always with me, and what's mine is yours. It was fitting to make merry and be glad, for this your brother was dead, and is alive; he was lost, and is found" (vv. 31–32).

Getting the Story Straight

At the start of this chapter, I noted that most of the great stories we can think of have something to do with homecoming—taking a meaningful journey. These great stories also include another element: transformation of the main character. The old men in *The Giving Tree* and "Death of the Hired Hand" have completed their journeys, having been transformed before the end. It is implied that the prodigal son's return will be accompanied by the resumption of his filial duties and by his willingness to abandon his old ways and live according to the rules of his father's house. He has already changed and will continue to change.

About 335 years before the birth of Christ, the ancient Greek philosopher Aristotle explained the way we all know this should work. In his famous treatise on literature, *Poetics*, he describes a character's transformation in terms of "reversal of fortune" and "discovery."[53] Furthermore, the main characters in any good story should have four attributes. They must be "good," "appropriate," "like the reality," and finally "consistent and the same throughout." Our evaluation of a good story is usually an unconscious or semi-conscious evaluation of whether the storyteller has gotten these traits right. We relate to the prodigal son because his reversal of fortune and discovery reveal all four of these elements of his character, and we identify with him without difficulty. The same happens in compelling real-world testimonies of people who have come to faith, as well as famous fairy tales or Oscar-winning movies.

On the first character trait, "goodness," even if the main character is a bad guy or an anti-hero, he is depicted in such a way that his actions evoke our pity, our fear, or our admiration. We recognize our own humanity in his and map our own journey onto his.

"Appropriate" is a category that still matters implicitly for most people, but many cultural offerings nowadays ask us to push our boundaries here. Aristotle's example of appropriateness happens to touch on a hot topic for us today. He notes, "The character before us may be, say, manly; but it is not appropriate in a female character to be manly." Like it or not, stereotypes are usually quite relatable.

Aristotle's third point, "like the reality," is an extension of the first two but a bit more contextual. Bad science fiction movies fail, for example, because the audience cannot keep track of all the invented deviations from normal human existence. Good ones succeed when a classic character arc and plot development just happen to take place in a galaxy far, far away.

The fourth, "consistent and the same throughout," is the trickiest part. We are interested in a character's change as a natural development. The discovery, therefore, is not of something brand new, but of something in the works just under the surface all along. The reversal of fortune is like a fertilizer or a catalyst.

Understanding why a person or a whole culture comes home to the Church is like understanding a great story of a transformative journey. With Aristotle's ancient principles in mind, we have a better framework for appreciating the way the grace of God works to elicit the fruit of seeds planted in every person, in every place, and at every time.

The story of anyone's entry into full communion with the Catholic Church is likely to have a fittingness to it. It is rare to hear the testimony of someone who abandons atheism or indifference one day and arrives at the baptismal font the next without a plot that that conforms in many respects to Aristotle's ancient definitions. At times, conversion stories have tragic elements—stories of hardship and loss of all kinds—but unlike *Oedipus Rex* or *King Lear*, they have a happy ending. Let us explore further.

"He Could Not Escape His Destiny"

I am afraid I must conjure St. John Henry Newman yet again. His homecoming to the ancient faith of Christ and his Church was a scandal in Victorian England, and he offers the modern world a special example of just how much Catholicism matters to the individual soul and to the good of the world.

Newman had spent twenty years as a cleric in the Church of England when he was compelled to give in and obey a call that he had been hearing for some time. His conversion was not just the resolution to an intellectual dilemma, but his understanding of becoming his true self in his true family. He was not escaping, but arriving.

Newman writes in his famous spiritual autobiography *Apologia Pro Vita Sua*,

> I am a Catholic by virtue of my believing in God; and if I am asked why I believe in God, I answer that it is because I believe in myself, for I feel it impossible to believe in my own existence . . . without believing also in the existence of him, who lives as a personal, all-seeing, all-judging being in my conscience.[54]

Newman came to believe that his own opinions about religion, although impeccably informed, put him in a dangerous position. He was acting as the arbiter of truth for himself, and therefore, he did not really understand who he was. It was up to him to judge whether something was of God or an inevitably flawed human musing. He was trying to build his own home as an escape from the one already prepared for him to dwell in.

Newman tells the story of coming home to the Church even more stirringly, and in entertaining conformity to Aristotle's norms, in his novel *Loss and Gain*. Published in 1845, the year Newman left the Church of England for the Catholic Church, the novel accomplishes what all good literature does. Taking a story out of the realm of the purely personal and dramatizing it makes the effect more universal. It's a book about a college kid trying to find out who he is and where he belongs—the same kind of scenario at the heart of the struggle between Yale undergraduates and their teachers in 2015.

Loss and Gain is the story of Charles Reading, the sensitive young son of an Anglican cleric. As his study of theology progresses at Oxford University, Charles is increasingly overwhelmed by the sense that the Catholic Church is his true home, and he needs to figure out how to get into it. The book is at times a hilarious slice of Victorian life, but it always insists upon the universal elements of compelling storytelling. Newman describes his novel's protagonist here in one florid, Romantic sentence:

> He could not escape the destiny, in due time, in God's time—though it might be long, though angels might be anxious, though the Church might plead as if defrauded of her promised increase of a stranger, yet a son; yet come it must, it was written in heaven, and the slow wheels of time each hour brought it nearer—he could not ultimately escape his destiny of becoming a Catholic.[55]

Charles is not escaping Protestantism or vice or society or anything else. Rather, his decision to become Catholic is his realization that there is no escape from what God has ordained.

All this may help explain why the Catholic Church does not officially use the term *convert* or *conversion* to describe people who leave a non-Catholic Christian group for the Catholic Church—people like Newman and his character, Charles Reading. People like me.

Once again, when I became Catholic, I was repeatedly welcomed "home," and this language is no accident. It accords perfectly with the Church's mission of "restoration," which I discussed in chapter two. When I became Catholic, I was not escaping my Protestant past, but bringing it to its destination, which welcomed my help in the ongoing restoration work.

The Catholic Church welcomes runaways, but it is not an escape. Rather, the Catholic Church is a place of freedom and responsibility; and ultimately, each Catholic must choose his own adventure within it.

CHAPTER 7

The Dictatorship Box

Even if someone agrees with me that the Catholic Church is no place to escape *to*, he may object that, on the contrary, it is somewhere to escape *from*. After all, the choice to belong to the Catholic Church was made for many by their parents and family members and, by extension, by the pressures of a wider Christian culture. A baby whose mother and father bring her to the Church for baptism obviously does not sign up for the system of sin and redemption on her own. It is a box people have been put in with no say of their own.

To critics of the modern bogeyman called Organized Religion—not to mention enemies of the final boss-level baddie that wears a miter and carries a pastoral staff—even adults who convert to the Catholic Church do so from a position of vulnerability. The Church may be big and beautiful, but does it not still hold us back from true freedom?

To some people, evangelism is always synonymous with coercion, and Church membership always has the look of a brainwashed cult. By extension, apologetics—particularly, explaining and defending the Faith for those who have fallen away from the Church—may seem to use the language of both love and liberty in a manipulative way. That is, how does God really love me the way churchmen tell me if he asks of me things that are too difficult, or things I do not understand? How am I free in Christ when the Church tells me I must live in a way that I do not prescribe for myself, and that conflicts at times with the identity I have constructed?

Conquered or Liberated?

In order to believe, some say, we must be willing not only to be dominated, but in effect to be annihilated—to surrender our human happiness for a vague promise of something better in an afterlife experience whose characteristics no two people are able to agree upon. From this perspective, the Church is a villain only pretending to have our best interest in mind. Fans of the Broadway musical *Hamilton* may conjure the image of King George III, who sings to the American revolutionaries, "When push comes to shove, I will send a fully armed battalion to remind you of my love!"

Another example from a more controversial source may be useful here.

On April 14, 2019, the medieval-feeling HBO series *Game of Thrones*, based on the novels of George R.R. Martin, aired its final episode to 19.3 million viewers in the United States. The week before, fans were horrified by the turn of Queen Daenerys Targaryen to tyrannical madness. As the city of King's Landing rang its bells in surrender, she spurred on her dragon and mercilessly torched innocent civilians and their homes. Dark stuff—a spine-tingling moment in a series that was often too gruesome and too obscene to tolerate.

In the end, Daenerys is motivated not primarily by the love of other as other, but by abstract ideas of liberty and justice. She anoints herself a savior and is willing to fight fire with fire until the unbearable weight of her own pain and pride makes her crazy. She deludes herself into thinking she can free people *from* oppression, but she has no vision of what they should be free *for*. As the dwarf Tyrion Lannister says to the exile Jon Snow in the final episode, "she'll go on liberating until all the peoples of the world are free, and she rules them all."

Daenerys's wickedness calls to mind the strategy of communist dictatorships in the twentieth century, and particularly the diabolical reign of Joseph Stalin in the Soviet Union. But critics or even just mild skeptics of the Catholic Church may point to elements in the story of Christian history as equally troubling. Once the Church had ascended to a place of power, did it not simply force people, even at the point of a sword or a gun, to receive the supposedly free gift of God's grace?

Yes and no.

Christians by Force?

There have indeed been moments in history when Christian leaders have forced conversion on non-Christians, or else presented them with an impossible dilemma of converting or facing blacklisting, deportation, or even death. One may think of Charlemagne's forced conversion of the Saxons in the late eighth century, or Vladimir the Great's order around the year 988 that the people of Kievan Rus be baptized *en masse* in the Dnieper River.

There are various accounts of forced conversions of Jews in the Rhineland, Bavaria, and other German lands in the High Middle Ages. In fifteenth-century Spain, there were not only forced conversions of Jews and Muslims, but also the expulsion of some "New Christians" suspected of merely pretending or even formally reverting to their previous religions. Forced conversion was sometimes attempted in the Americas, although rarely successfully, during the colonial era. More recently, there is the famous case of Edgardo Mortara, who, in 1858, was taken away from his Jewish family after it became known that a housemaid had secretly baptized him.

History is full of both great and not-so-great accounts of Christians' behavior on account of their faith. And modern people may bristle at the idea that fully Christian civilizations required adherence to Christian doctrine and morality in the same way that liberal societies now require that everyone toe the line on matters of gender and sexuality, to name just two high-profile issues. Nonetheless, the Church has stated clearly in recent times that forced conversion is a no-no. In his 1975 encyclical on evangelism, *Evangelii Nuntiandi*, Pope St. Paul VI wrote,

> The Church cannot accept violence, especially the force of arms—which is uncontrollable once it is let loose—and indiscriminate death as the path to liberation, because it knows that violence always provokes violence and irresistibly engenders new forms of oppression and enslavement that are often harder to bear than those from which they claimed to bring freedom.

Whatever coercive practices may have been used in the past should not continue in the Church today.

Living For and Dying For

Do you ever stop and think how many lives were lost to achieve noble ends? If you visit the haunted battlefield of Gettysburg, you will learn that about 51,000 soldiers died on both sides of that Union victory.[56] You may also learn that those casualties were just a fraction of the 620,000 soldiers who died in all the battles of the Civil War. The result: Chattel slavery on American soil was brought to an end.

Likewise, in World War II, my grandfather on my mother's side was at the Battle of Anzio, which featured some of the fiercest fighting of the war, and later he was at the Battle of the Bulge, where 80,000 American soldiers were killed, wounded or captured, or went missing.[57] On my father's side, my grandfather was at Pearl Harbor at the beginning of the war and Tokyo Bay at the end, with a dozen other major sea battles in between. Stopping the madness of the Axis Powers' (and particularly Hitler's) conquests culminated in 15 million total battle deaths (not to mention all the civilian casualties, including the extermination of 6 million Jews).[58] And the risk my family members took for their country and for a wider mission to help people in need was entirely warranted.

The point is that in the memory of many of us alive today in the West, there have been things of monumental importance worth dying for. And as I mentioned in chapter four, in parts of Africa, Asia, and elsewhere, people still die for the sake of the gospel today. Martyrdom is not a thing of the past, nor has heroic service to our fellow man fallen away with the advent of cyber-warfare or drone attacks. Nor again have the utopian ideals of the United Nations eliminated the real prospect that every new generation may have to sacrifice some of its first fruits in order that future generations get to live.

There is a longing in the human spirit to care so much about something important that one would even be willing to die for it. Sadly, in a world that dissuades us from thinking that *anything* is worth dying for—let alone a stuffy old religion— people sometimes sacrifice their lives for something unworthy of their God-given dignity. Even in the darkness of the hearts of terrorists, there lies some perverse notion of goodness, of sacrificing for a (misperceived, in this case) greater purpose.

Death: Dictator or Liberator?

As twentieth-century bloodshed testifies to those of us with eyes to see, humans cannot flourish under and therefore will not tolerate long-term oppression. The Church that Christ founded would never exist today if the Faith rested on the strength of men alone. Rather, to become and to remain a Christian is to choose individually and collectively to find perfect freedom in this life under the lordship of Christ the King. And although Christianity has both flourished and struggled under a variety of human political arrangements, with leaders possessing strength ranging from a figurehead to a tyrant, Christians ultimately proclaim that Jesus is Lord, and that every chieftain, king, emperor, president, and prime minister is not. How, then, do we choose our ultimate freedom in Christ in a world that wants our ultimate allegiance in myriad ways?

One way is to think more about death.

Today, death has become the greatest of all dictators. As such, death must be avoided—indeed, we are taught to flee from it and fight it for as long as possible, until scientists achieve the ultimate innovation of defeating it for good. When death inevitably comes, and especially when it comes sooner than expected, a person may experience it not just as the evil byproduct of man's sin that the Christian believes it to be, but instead as a cosmic betrayal from a cruel regime of nature that men must overthrow.

The virtue of Christian hope, however, puts death into its proper context. Pope Benedict XVI began his encyclical *Spe Salvi* (Saved in Hope) this way: "The present, even if it is arduous, can be lived and accepted if it leads toward a goal, if we can be sure of this goal, and if this goal is great enough to justify the effort of the journey." So how can we be sure of this goal, thereby living lives of freedom in the Church in anticipation of eternal life with God? To answer this question, I turn to a French philosopher by way of a French filmmaker.

The Wager

Until his death in 2010, Eric Rohmer was one of the major figures of European cinema, directing twenty-five feature films in a forty-five-year span and serving for a time as the editor of *Cahiers du Cinéma*, the influential publication of the French New Wave. He was also a lifelong practicing Catholic whose films are charming and quirky, steeped in philosophy, and depicting people's commitments to living according to religious or ethical principles. Many of Rohmer's protagonists navigate the secular minefields of hedonism and relativism with their ideals intact, finally experiencing an otherworldly joy—neither happiness nor sadness, but a sometimes-unwitting experience of satisfaction before God.

In 1965, Rohmer directed a program for French television called *Entretien sur Pascal* (On Pascal), featuring a cordial debate between two philosophers: an atheist, Brice Parain, and a Dominican priest, Fr. Dominique Dubarle. Pascal was a seventeenth-century mathematician, scientist, and philosopher whose "brilliant and inquisitve mind" Pope Francis celebrated in his 2023 apostolic letter *Sublimitas et Miseria Hominis* (On the Grandeur and Misery of Man), which marked the four-hundredth anniversary of Pascal's birth.

From the televised conversation sprang the idea for a major component of Rohmer's 1969 masterpiece *My Night at Maud's*, which focuses on Pascal's famous wager, as described in his *Pensées*. In simplified form, Pascal's wager is meant "to incite to the search after God,"[59] and it describes how a person ought to live as if God exists, since if God does not exist, the worst-case scenario will be a finite, material loss rather than the loss of his soul.

My Night at Maud's is the third installment of Rohmer's "Six Moral Tales."[60] It tells the story of a young Catholic engineer, Jean-Louis, played by Jean-Louis Trintignant, who recently began a quiet life working for Michelin in the central French city of Clermont-Ferrand, Pascal's hometown. After several years living abroad, Jean-Louis has had love affairs and even lived with women, but he is determined to abandon his old behavior and find a Catholic wife. He tells his work colleagues reticently, "My family was Catholic, and I've kept it up," but he later admits more enthusiastically to his friends, "I'm a convert."

The film begins at Mass, where Jean-Louis spots a young woman named Françoise, played by Marie-Christine Barrault, who "was truly Catholic and had just emerged from a convent."[61] Jean-Louis attempts to follow Françoise with his car, finally seeing her again, and declaring "on that day, I knew that Françoise would be my wife." But before Jean-Louis can arrange a way to meet Françoise, he bumps into an old friend, Vidal, an atheist Marxist, who explains how he appreciates Pascal's wager for his own view of the meaning of history. That is, the promise of creating a left-wing Utopia on earth is so wonderful—however improbable—that it is a good bet to believe the tenets of Marxism rather than to resist them. Jean-Louis does not buy it, and Vittorio Hösle notes that Vidal's appropriation of Pascal's philosophy serves only "to discredit it in Rohmer's eyes."[62] How can one trust a theory about the freedom to choose eternity with Christ if it can be so easily repurposed for worldly ends?

Vidal agrees to tag along to Christmas Eve Mass, where Jean-Louis's experience of almost supernatural certainty about his future is affirmed in the words of the priest's homily, which was delivered by a real Dominican priest, Father Guy Léger, "a movie lover who returned to his monastery at the end of his day on the set."[63] Emphasizing "the living joy" of the power of Christ in every human heart, the homily sets both a challenge and opportunity in front of Jean-Louis as he pursues his goal of winning the heart of Françoise and starting his own Catholic family.

But no sooner does Jean-Louis acquire a clear vision of joy than he finds himself in danger of abandoning it. After Mass, he and Vidal pay a visit to the beautiful divorcée Maud, played by Françoise Fabian. Maud is an agnostic physician, a single mother, and a secular free thinker, who hosts Jean-Louis and Vidal to a simple supper. The men's conversation about Pascal resumes, with Maud joining in, expressing curiosity about how Jean-Louis can identify as a Catholic and yet reject Pascal for being too rigorous. After all, Catholics seem to have an awful lot of rules. Jean-Louis declares, "If that's what Christianity is, then I'm an atheist," asserting that on the contrary, the informal norms of secularism are bound by more rigidity and governed by stricter principles than Christianity. Rohmer himself said about those who put their "faith in the left" in an interview with *Cahiers du Cinéma* in 1965, "I'm free, it seems to me! But people aren't."

Rejecting the Puritan tendencies of secularism, Marxism, and certain versions of Christianity, Jean-Louis holds up the example of food and drink, wondering what Pascal would have thought of an earlier vintage of the same local wine they are enjoying. Jean-Louis slaps the table, points to his glass, and declares, "That's it! Me, I say, 'This, this is good!'" To Jean-Louis and to Catholics at all times and places, authentic Christianity ought to be the experience of an abundant reality, not an insurance policy against hellfire.

But remaining faithful is still an enormous challenge that feels, at times, like a burden.

In the film, Jean-Louis no sooner proclaims his freedom to enjoy life as a Catholic than he is presented with a real test of his moral resolve. He is forced to wonder: What are the limits of freedom for a Christian? Where does enjoyment of the gifts of God's creation stop and indulgence in deadly sin begin? Rohmer depicts Jean-Louis and Maud alone in a long, tense scene in which the viewer wonders whether chastity or debauchery will win out. Jean-Louis's chaste resolve appears to fail just as Maud grows tired of the game, and the frigid night gives way to warm sun coming through the windows. In the darkness, Jean-Louis has explored the moral landscape right up to its furthest limit, and until the last minute, but without transgressing. A reader of the Bible may recall the Psalmist's declaration: "Joy comes with the morning" (Ps. 30:5).

Jean-Louis approaches Françoise the next day, and the new couple experience their own wintry night, stranded indoors together. But whereas intellectual debate and sexual tension dominated Jean-Louis's night with Maud, pleasant theological *badinage* between fellow believers, as well as the total presumption of chastity, characterizes his night with Françoise. The next morning, the two attend Mass together, and the priest says in his homily that Christianity is not mere morality, "but life." Just as Jean-Louis has foreseen, the couple marry, beginning the next phase of a wholesome, joyous life with God together after confessing to each other the sins of their past.

Here we see how Pascal's wager works, and why the free choice of faith offers the greatest liberation. We can be free as a Christian or a slave as anything else. Leszek Kolakowski notes that "Pascal appeals to a kind of practical reasoning in order to compel the libertine to admit that he cannot avoid the choice between religion and irreligion."[64] In *My Night at Maud's*, Both Jean-Louis and Maud are, or were, libertines—but he chooses religion, and she chooses irreligion. In the end, Rohmer makes clear who made the better decision.

In the final scene of the film, the hibernal setting has changed to a mild summer scene, as Jean-Louis, Françoise, and their little son bump into Maud at the beach, five years after the famous night. Jean-Louis hangs back and talks to her alone, and Maud tells him that she has married for a second time and is now facing a second divorce. She is as beautiful as ever, but sad, implying to Jean-Louis that Françoise had

had an affair with Maud's first husband before Jean-Louis met her. Despite this revelation, Jean-Louis radiates contentment, returning to his wife, whose countenance has become grim. Perceiving that Françoise is ashamed of the adulterous behavior of her past, Jean-Louis lets her believe that he had given into temptation with Maud all those years ago in a "final escapade." Suddenly, Françoise's joy returns, and the little Catholic family runs toward the sea, smiling and laughing.

Rohmer would return to Pascal's wager in a much later film, *A Tale of Winter* (1992). In more than two dozen feature films over the course of his career, he depicted characters wrestling with philosophical dilemmas, but ultimately avoiding the dictatorship of base carnal desires. Thankfully, Rohmer's commitment to his Catholic faith kept him away from the despair that so many of his contemporaries explored on screen, and his work holds its own against—if not exceeds—the aesthetic and intellectual achievements of his peers.[65]

Back to Church

Catholics have long understood that the basic concepts of sin and forgiveness are meaningless without a living authority to define and administer God's life-giving law. As a Protestant, I had no assurance that I was ever living in a state of freedom—or not—from the bonds of my sin. For example, was it enough for me to "feel" forgiven? I came to believe that it was not.

Some of my Catholic friends are surprised when I tell them that there are approved rites for reconciliation in many Anglican ecclesial bodies, including the Episcopal Church, which was the jurisdiction I served for almost ten years. However, very few Anglicans make use of these rites, and even if they choose to do so, it is only a personal matter. There is a long-standing slogan among Anglicans with regard to reconciliation that goes something like this: "All may, none must, some should."

What a mess! If I am "free" to have a clergyman pronounce God's forgiveness of my sins, how am I equally free from those sins if I choose to mention them to God alone? Moreover, how am I free from sins if I do not have a clear judgment from the Church about what constitutes a sin? As a Catholic, I now find the sacrament of reconciliation the setting of man's greatest liberation on this side of eternity—like the Church itself, the confessional is a little place that is much bigger on the inside!

More generally, as a Catholic now, it is clear to me that the best priests and bishops, let alone the best popes, are anything but authoritarian leaders. Even in the context of the sacrament of reconciliation, their authority to bind and loose comes from Christ, and they too must make recourse to the sacrament as regularly as any other Catholic. The ministry of men in collars, then, is not about telling people what to do, but rather about assessing and affirming the work being undertaken by the other members of the body of Christ. The body needs a head, but heads do not walk or lift or stretch. Heads cannot even speak without their connections to the lungs and vocal cords.

The choice to come to belong to the Church, or to remain within it, or to come back to it, is therefore not just a choice to acknowledge clergymen as spiritual authorities. Nor is being Catholic a matter of mere obedience to orders. Nor again is life as a Catholic anything like blind adherence, brainless submission, or a foolhardy spirit of going along to get along. As Pascal teaches us and Rohmer illustrates on screen, our faith is a choice upon which eternity depends—but just as importantly, it is how one experiences himself as being most human in the world.

Nonetheless, funny, false assumptions persist about the almost slave-like conditions under which Catholics must toil in the world.

Dogma: How Loud?

My Southern Baptist grandmother switched from the Democrats to the Republicans in 1960 because she believed that if John F. Kennedy became president, he would have to take orders from the pope. More recently, some progressive secular types believed that when the Catholic jurist Amy Coney Barrett was nominated to be a justice of the Supreme Court, she would be judging matters of state as a brainwashed stooge not only of the Magisterium, but also of a charismatic group to which she belonged called People of Praise.

Barrett's story bears a little more examination.

In 2017, a few years before her nomination to the Supreme Court, Barrett appeared before the United States Senate for a confirmation hearing to a federal judgeship. During this process, Senator Dianne Feinstein famously said to Barrett, "The dogma lives loudly within you, and that is a concern." Almost overnight, traditional Catholics began to wear Feinstein's words as a badge of honor, emblazoning them on merchandise like t-shirts and stickers. And indeed, Feinstein's words appeared to say the quiet part of progressive prejudice out loud—that is, even though secular people pay lip service to the beliefs of traditional Christians, they are really looking for ways to diminish or disqualify us because of our faith commitments.

On another level, however, Feinstein's words point to a more general paranoia among nonbelievers about the possibility of Catholics and other Christians seeking to grow the ranks of religious slavery. Even after Barrett's eventual confirmation, groups of women dressed in red "handmaid" outfits protested outside Barrett's home in homage to Margaret Atwood's novel *A Handmaid's Tale*, which proposes a dystopian future where women are forced to become pregnant and give birth. To Barrett's critics, the mere fact of her adherence to the Church's teaching on the subject of abortion was considered unacceptable for a life of public service.

Our old friend St. John Henry Newman helps us reset the terms of this kind of discourse. In his *Letter to the Duke of Norfolk* of 1875, Newman sought to defend the primacy of conscience in the life of Catholics living in non-Catholic contexts. Much of his discussion is specific to the peculiar situation of confessing Catholics taking part in the life of an established Protestant country, but, as always with Newman, his argument touches on universal principles that are useful to Catholics always and everywhere.

To start with, Newman quips that the civil authorities of his day are not really concerned that Catholics have a weird theology that requires allegiance to a foreign ecclesiastical power. Rather, he tells us, "it is not the existence of a pope, but of a Church" that is the real problem.[66] That is, the world seems to hate it that Catholics point backward in continuity with a source of truth that transcends today's latest thing, whatever it may be. Almost evoking today's slang, Newman calls such critics "haters of Catholicism"—that is, people with no good arguments and a nonsensical aversion.[67]

The most important chapters from the *Letter to the Duke of Norfolk* came as a real shock to the people in Newman's day who assumed that Catholics are sniveling automatons of a celibate Italian in a fancy gown. First noting that the pope does not make Vatican decrees, but rather vice versa, Newman argued that there is necessarily something in human beings that ensures no possibility of enslavement to the false teachings of any authority, be he ecclesiastical or temporal:

the human conscience. Because of the conscience, which he calls "the aboriginal vicar of Christ," no man can give absolute obedience either to a pope or to a monarch. Newman concludes his chapter on conscience with the famous line: "If I am obliged to bring religion into after-dinner toasts . . . I shall drink—to the pope, if you please—still, to conscience first, and to the pope afterwards."

Newman's remark should in no way be taken to mean that my opinions could stand in judgment of Church teaching. Just the opposite. Indeed, the scourge of "private judgment" is one of the major reasons Newman chose to come into full communion with the Catholic Church in the first place. And he spoke in various places about a larger hope of a return to baptized society that would be possible only as the Catholic Church reclaimed its role in Europe as the organizing principle for everyone's lives. Nonetheless, Newman's insistence on the primacy of conscience has been for many deeply committed Catholics the assurance of freedom in Christ that makes any naysayers' epithets about brainwashing or coercion seem absurd. As Pascal says in introducing his wager, "Do not then condemn as wrong those who have made a choice, for you know nothing about it."[68]

Freedom of the Saints

For people who are still unconvinced that being a Catholic is the path to freedom, not bondage, the lives of the saints often bear witness to the fact that God deals directly through the consciences of his faithful people. Moreover, the most dynamic movements and most exciting moments in the renewal of the Faith come from the bottom up, not the top down. The Church, being divinely instituted and maintained, has always had the flexibility to face the truth, even when it comes from unlikely sources.

One such source is St. Joan of Arc. Joan cared deeply about her country, France, which had been embroiled in the Hundred Years' War with England for as long as anyone could remember. As a teenager she received visions of St. Michael the Archangel, the patron saint of the area where she lived, long revered among all French people. She also had visions of St. Margaret of Antioch and St. Catherine of Alexandria, both virgin martyrs from the early Church. In swift succession, Joan demanded and was granted an audience with the rightful but uncrowned king of France, Charles VII, who sent her away to theologians to ensure that she was a pious Catholic and no kook. In April of 1429, Joan defied all expectations and led the French army in lifting the English siege on the city of Orleans, being wounded by an arrow in the process.

The many other amazing adventures of Joan of Arc are well worth studying, but for our purposes, the end of Joan's earthly story is most illustrative. Her faithfulness unto death shows us how her Catholic faith ensured her perfect freedom when the world did its worst to her. She was literally being oppressed and dominated, a victim of grave injustice, and she knew exactly what she was about. Almost five centuries later, the Church agreed, as Pope Benedict XV canonized her a saint.

Another, more recent example may make the point even more clearly. Franz Jägerstätter led no armies and spoke to no kings. He was a simple Austrian farmer who took his Catholic faith so seriously that he refused to swear allegiance to Hitler—the ultimate dictator—and found himself in prison, far from his family. Like Joan, he was put to death as a martyr, and he is now a Blessed, *en route* to canonization, God willing. In Terence Mallick's 2019 film *A Hidden Life*, Jägerstätter's lawyer offers him one last chance to be released from prison and avoid the executioner's blade. He will be spared combat duty and will likely live out the war and return to his family, as long as he says the perfunctory oath and binds himself to the Führer. Jägerstätter's lawyer tells him he doesn't really have to *mean* what he says in the words of the oath. He'll go free. "But I am free," Jägerstätter replies.

The life of Christ in the Catholic Church is an indictment of every counterfeit form of human freedom. Whether one is baptized into the Faith as a baby or chooses initiation with the aid of rational faculties as an adult, freedom in Christ is a great gift to be received. The straitjackets and iron bars are all *out there* from the Church's perspective, not *in here*.

Nonetheless, being Catholic is hard. And in the next chapter, we must finally take a realistic look at the challenges of life as a Catholic.

CHAPTER 8

The Preference Box

It is an almost impossible question: What would you include or exclude if you were creating your own religion? What do you prefer to see in your Church unboxing, as you might prefer in a cosmetics or shoe unboxing? What would you click away from?

The word *religion* necessarily conjures up the idea of a system of beliefs and practices that we do not, indeed cannot, make up. And with rare exceptions among genuine psychopaths or the most ardent ideologues, even people who explicitly eschew established religions piece together for themselves a way of living that appeals to truths outside themselves. Everyone, everywhere experiences some pressure to conform to ideas of right and wrong.

Therefore, despite the expansive space and liberating feeling of the Catholic faith that I tried to convey in previous chapters, it is important as we near the end of our study to say this plainly: being Catholic is hard. There can be no sugarcoating it. In many respects, a person would be crazy to prefer it to other options—and indeed, in the world today, most people don't.

But the Catholic Church is not a preference . . . and for that reason, it offers the best way to live.

Who Decides?

In an oft-memed scene from the Coen Brothers' 1999 film *The Big Lebowski*, there is an altercation in a bowling alley with an ex-con named Jesus (pronounced the Spanish way), who unleashes a torrent of obscene taunting on the protagonist, who calls himself the Dude, played by Jeff Bridges. Leaning back with his arms over his head, the Dude looks at his foul-mouthed interlocutor and quips, "Well, you know, that's just, like, your opinion, man." By contrast, throughout the film, the Dude's bowling teammate and buddy, Walter, played by John Goodman, dismisses the relevance of opinions entirely. Incidentally, Walter's mouth may be fouler than the afore-mentioned Jesus', but he considers himself a man of principle: although raised Catholic, he clings fervently to the Jewish faith of his ex-wife, refusing to bowl or do any other activity on the Sabbath. And when the Dude rebukes him—"You're not even Jewish, man! You're Polish Catholic!"—Walter, however bombastically, nonetheless shows that his friend's rejection of the principles he's taken on has cut him to the heart.

It is an interesting element of Walter's character that he has not found enough rigor in his own Catholic upbringing—or at any rate, he has taken well to the rigor he discovered in the variety of Judaism he has come to know. The Catholic Church does caricature itself at times by projecting a legalism with endless exceptions. A silly monologue by the character of Brother Geraghty, played by Chris O'Dowd, in the 2014 film *St. Vincent* illustrates the point. Welcoming a new student to class, Brother Geraghty, a religion teacher in a Catholic school, explains that all religions and none are welcome, but he concludes, "I'm a Catholic, which is the best of all the religions, really, because we have the most rules."

As a Catholic, I chuckle with my fellow Catholics at Brother Geraghty's words, but as a former Protestant who gave up a

THE PREFERENCE BOX

pretty comfortable life to become Catholic, I am also a little annoyed with them. I am annoyed because I know some of my fellow Catholics think of their faith in this same nonsensical preferential way as Brother Geraghty. On the other hand, legalism *per se*, like the more intense forms of Orthodox Judaism that *The Big Lebowski* amusingly critiques in the character of Walter, is not quite what we are after, either.

Crossing the Tiber

When people are baptized into the Catholic Church or come into full communion with the Catholic Church from another Christian group, it is sometimes referred to as "crossing the Tiber" or "swimming the Tiber." The Tiber is the river that flows through Rome, so the expression is a symbol of making one's way through worldly obstacles to the Catholic Church. It may be self-evident that such a move is a big deal, but I often feel the need to convey just how big a deal it really is.

As I have mentioned in various ways, the only unifying principle for the disparate non-Catholic groups is that none of them is (Roman) Catholic. Thus, even a liturgically sky-high Anglican is ultimately someone whose spiritual authority rests in some debatable combination of his own biblical interpretation and interaction with traditions of Christians from different eras. Some Protestants may be *sola scriptura* types; others heavily emphasize being "creedal"; others have devised an authority structure based on voting; others use images like a three-legged stool of Scripture, Tradition, and Reason; others are proudly non-creedal, and anything goes. It may be possible to be excluded from fellowship with a particular group, but there is likely another group more than willing to take you in. Indeed, the main growth strategy of some Protestant groups may be to offer themselves as an alternative to other congregations that are perceived to be either too liberal or too conservative. Atheism has its own appeals—namely, *every* religion is wrong. Agnosticism seems to grow with no deliberate cultivation whatever.

Being Catholic is a different experience, and the image of crossing over from one side of a river to another is therefore apt. To become Catholic is to be somewhere else, even if one's old home is still plainly in view. And nowhere is this change more readily apparent than in the simple matter of upholding the Catholic Church's precepts, the first of which requires Catholics to attend Mass on Sundays and on holy days of obligation under penalty of sin. It is simply required of us, as the *Catechism* says, "to sanctify the day commemorating the resurrection of the Lord as well as the principal liturgical feasts honoring the mysteries of the Lord, the Blessed Virgin Mary, and the saints" (2042). The *Catechism* is also clear about circumstances that can legitimately dispense us from our obligation to attend Mass, but the obligation remains.

It really is beyond comprehension for a Protestant to be told that he must go to church or else face damnation. The Sabbath was made for man, not man for the Sabbath, they might say, quoting Mark 2. Going to church is important, but it is not the end of the world to miss it. And indeed, since God alone knows the hearts of the faithful, it may be that the redneck on his bass boat on a Sunday morning is in better spiritual shape than the prim and proper widow who is riding a 520-week church attendance streak. The aversion to being told we must go to church as an obligation is shared by non-Catholics of every variety, whether conservative, liberal, or something in between.

It may take some time, even after becoming Catholic, for a newcomer to wrap his mind around the idea that the Church requires of me what is necessary for me. It is precisely because we cannot know the hearts of people that all of Christ's followers must submit to the same discipline, with the same hope for growth in holiness. It is not about belonging to the Church of the overachiever, with the most rules providing the most opportunities for success. Rather, it is the opposite: creating a baseline for everyone seeking God's grace. There are no preferences for anyone; rather, there are sacrifices with ultimate benefits for everyone.

Nonetheless, even for lifelong Catholics, it can seem like a chore to keep the first precept. Every seven days rolls around pretty quickly, and there are always potential excuses.

Sin, More Generally

Willingly refusing to attend Mass when one is otherwise able is just one example of a mortal sin that requires the sacrament of reconciliation to remove from one's soul. Here too, even after becoming Catholic, a new Catholic may continue to bristle for a while.

Protestants know of no such distinction between *mortal* and *venial*, and non-Christians may find the whole framework of sin absurd . . . and the prospect of saying sins out loud to a man in a box positively perverse!

But absurd and perverse, that is, only where an act is widely perceived not to hurt anybody. If I stopped a Baptist or an atheist on the street and asked, "Do you think it is appropriate for a murderer to go to confession?", both might be inclined to answer in the affirmative, even though they both officially have no use for confession. But if I asked, "Do you think someone ought to go to confession for masturbating?", both would likely refuse, and passionately. Even if such an act were deemed wrong—a big if—it's nobody's business but God's. And God is certainly not going to cast someone away for a solitary act that imposes nothing on anyone else.

In my experience, however, a person truly seeking God is likely to reach a breaking point on the question of how to deal with sin. Something seemingly as trivial as masturbation is a good case in point. The sexual act is pleasurable because it is meant to be experienced for an intended purpose: the potential procreation of children between a married couple. When that pleasure is detached from its purpose, it becomes an obstacle to communion with God and to an individual's full human flourishing.

If we are God's and not our own, then even these "private" matters carry eternal consequences. And so either we find or invent a system outside ourselves to deal with sin—e.g., the sacrament of reconciliation for Catholics or an accountability partner for Evangelicals—or else we give up on the objective reality of sin and settle for relativism.

The latter option leans heavily into the Protestant notion of personal revelation, personal relationship, and individual salvation. It also cherry-picks words of Christ, at times even pitting Christ against either an imagined Old Testament tyrant god or a "Church" god whose origin story may begin with the Pharisees, or maybe with Paul, or maybe with the Emperor Constantine, or who knows whom else depending on whom one asks. In this mindset, *obviously* Jesus doesn't care what a man does alone in his bedroom or what two consenting adults do in theirs. *Obviously,* God just wants people to be nice to one another.

Thus, sometimes people who are serious about trying not to sin, and particularly people who make use of the Church's system for removing sin, are caricatured as being somehow privileged. For example, if a person happens not to be attracted to someone of the same sex or happens not to find drug use appealing or happens not to feel compelled to gamble—or, God willing, all of the above and more!—then he places unrealistic expectations on others who do struggle in those ways. That is, there cannot possibly be a universal standard for behavior that falls into a category like "mortal sin" when everyone is born different and has myriad life experiences that create different moral norms.

It is painfully evident, however, that it is fairly difficult for most people not to sin. No one is naturally "privileged" in this regard. For my part, I tried as a Protestant for a long time to rationalize some of my own shortcomings while at the same time beating myself up unduly over other ones. I did, therefore, become privileged, in a manner of speaking, when I surrendered all of this nonsense and agreed to live my life within the sacramental system of the Catholic Church, just like every other Catholic, with every other strength and weakness imaginable down through the ages to the present moment.

To many in the world, however, choosing the Catholic Church as the best way to deal with one's sin is still a preference. And indeed, when my family and I came into full communion with the Catholic Church, there were more than a few Protestant and non-religious friends who congratulated us for finding the right fit for our pre-existing views.

In fact, what we chose to do by becoming Catholic made our lives much harder! But entirely worth it.

Marriage Problems

A huge stumbling block for some people to enter the Catholic Church, to stay in the Catholic Church, or even to understand the Catholic Church has to do with marriage.

When I was an Episcopal priest preparing couples for marriage, I would always begin by telling them that they needed to think of their wedding day as a starting block rather than a finish line. This image would have been unnecessary in generations past, where most weddings were lovely affairs, but they rarely required large bank loans to finance and never involved a "destination." For anyone my age and older, our parents' wedding photos look modest—a church of some kind, a piece of cake and a glass of champagne in the hall next door, and perhaps a band and some dancing if they were well heeled or well connected. There were no reality television shows about wedding planning, but also, most everyone got married and stayed married, "for better or for worse."

The "for worse" part is important, as marriage has always required enormous sacrifice from both the man and the woman. There have always been situations where it was unsafe or simply impossible for a man and woman bound by marriage vows to continue to live under the same roof. Moreover, in the Catholic context, there have always been marriages that were discovered later to be *invalid* because the bride or the groom—or both—did not enter into the marriage sincerely. Hence, annulment exists.

But the vows themselves, if entered into validly, are always meant to ensure that when the initial enthusiasm of young love transitions into the daily grind of family life, the marriage itself does not morph into a preference to be continued or ended. As I also used to tell couples preparing for marriage: You really don't know whom you're marrying. Therefore, the whole reason you make a promise is so that when it's hard to keep it, you have to.

I dwell on marriage here because it is one area of Catholic teaching that the world struggles especially to understand, and it presents a real challenge to Catholics seeking to live faithfully. Like the matter of having to go to confession, having to be in a valid Catholic marriage (if not in a state of celibacy) in order to participate fully in the life of the Church can seem positively cruel. After all, there are an awful lot of divorced people out there in the world today. They would certainly prefer if the Church affirmed them in the way they feel they deserve. But again, being Catholic is not about preferences.

Few if any non-Catholics would understand, for example, the existence of people called "heroic standers," a term coined by Daniel and Bethany Meola, founders of Life-Giving Wounds, an apostolate focused on healing for adult children of divorce.[69] These "standers" are people who have, for various reasons, ended up abandoned by their spouses, but they have pledged not to remarry civilly or seek annulment from the Church. Instead, they honor their marriage vows against all odds, praying for reconciliation with the spouses who have wronged them and being generous to their children, grandchildren, and friends. "They demonstrate," Dan and Bethany explain, "the fruitfulness of marital vows even in the midst of suffering and a lack of reciprocity."

Perhaps even fewer people would sympathize with a friend of mine who attends Mass every day and yet has not received Communion for more than twenty years. The reason is that his marriage blew up, and he drifted away from the Church before getting into a civil arrangement—a "remarriage," according to the rest of the world—with a woman he loves with all his heart. Many people in my friend's circumstances would likely have ended up in a Protestant pew (at best), or more likely would have abandoned Christianity entirely as a member of the large religious group known as "ex-Catholics." Instead, in time, my friend was drawn back to the truth of the Catholic faith—but this truth now makes a heavy demand of him. Because marriage is a sacrament and therefore permanent, my friend lives in an impaired state of communion unless or until he is able to make regular his situation—be it by receiving from the Church a declaration of nullity for the marriage he contracted so long ago, or by leaving his current life and returning to that marriage, which the Church teaches must be presumed valid unless proven otherwise. And so, not yet having achieved either of those outcomes, he shows up humbly, every day, penitential for the mistakes of his past and hopeful for the outpouring of God's grace—on God's terms—in his future.

On a purely emotional level, my friend's *preference* would be for the Church to say it doesn't really matter. But if he got his way, my friend would always wonder what else the Church has taught him to believe that doesn't really matter. My friend is not interested in "your opinion, man," or in his own opinion, either. He also does not merely have a morbid fascination with rules. Rather, he prays by himself in the pew while almost everyone else goes up to receive the body of Christ, because God is God, and he is not. As Henri de Lubac wrote of the Catholic, "his submission in consequence is not an abdication, his orthodoxy is not mere conformity, but fidelity."[70]

United to the divorced person who accepts the reality of truth with regard to marriage is the same-sex-attracted person who refuses the world's overwhelming encouragement to live as he sees fit. United to them both is the person with gender dysphoria who eschews hormones and surgeries and seeks hope to get through the day-to-day struggles of feeling out of place. United too is the young woman who refuses to have an abortion, the young man who quits pornography, the young couple who refuse birth control and open themselves to life, heedless of the world's pressures for careers and financial security, let alone financial success. United to them all is every faithful Catholic, every day, who would prefer some things be like this instead of like that—people who seek God's grace to think bigger than their individual desires, and who are unashamed to go on seeking holiness even though sin compromises everything in their lives.

Being Catholic is hard, and a privilege. Real life.

No Politics, Please

I mentioned earlier that my maternal grandmother, whose parents and siblings were solid New Deal Southern Democrats, changed party affiliation in 1960 because she was worried that a Catholic president would be primarily answerable to the pope. (At any rate, that is the family lore.) Over the next few decades, she and my grandfather would feel more comfortable in the Republican Party in the wake of the social upheavals of the late 1960s, the legalization of abortion, and concerns about religious freedom. My grandparents were illustrative of changing political affiliation among Christians in America, Protestant and Catholic alike.

American Catholics used to be counted on as a solid bloc of the Democrat coalition, which included working-class whites, blacks, and immigrants. As late as when I was a teenager in 1996, 53 percent of Catholics voted for President Bill Clinton, compared to 37 percent for Senator Bob Dole, increasing Clinton's share of the Catholic vote compared to his first election in 1992.[71] According to *America* magazine, the Catholic vote went narrowly for George W. Bush over John Kerry (a Catholic) in 2004, but it went back to the Democrat, Barack Obama, in 2008.[72] In 2016, Catholics voted 52 percent in favor of Donald Trump compared to 44 percent for Hillary Clinton. And according to Gallup News, Trump and Biden (a Catholic) effectively split the Catholic vote evenly in 2020.[73]

Back in the 1990s, President Clinton spoke of abortion as something that should be "safe, legal, and rare"—conflicting with Catholic teaching, but paying lip service to the fact that people who voted for him thought abortion should not be happening at all. Today, even though some baptized Catholics continue to waffle between Democrat and Republican, the matters of not only abortion, but also marriage, transgenderism, and other issues that are now non-negotiable on the left have put Catholic leaders in a more difficult position. Moreover, it has become more difficult for Catholics who pay close attention to Catholic teaching to settle for a "you say *potayto*, I say *potahto*" approach to politics.

On May 20, 2022, Archbishop Salvatore Cordileone of San Francisco issued a pastoral letter that may be remembered as a turning point in American Catholic life. After explaining his attempts to get clarity on the abortion position of Nancy Pelosi, a Catholic under his authority as well as the speaker of the United States House of Representatives, he was left with a difficult decision to make. He wrote, "I must make a public declaration that she is not to be admitted to Holy Communion unless and until she publicly repudiate her support for abortion 'rights' and confess and receive absolution for her cooperation in this evil in the sacrament of penance."[74]

Now, Archbishop Cordileone did not say it is a sin to vote for a Democrat, or indeed that one must or even should vote for a Republican. But he did single out a core plank of the Democrat platform, which, if publicly championed, would henceforth be considered a deal-breaker for a person desiring full participation in the life of the Catholic Church.

Controversy remains about the status of Archbishop Cordileone's injunction as it pertains to other people in other places, and Pope Francis did not buttress Cordileone's words with his own words of clarity on the matter. Nonetheless, whatever grasp left-of-center political parties and movements had on Catholics has now morphed into a grasp on Catholics who wish Catholicism were something other than what it is.

This sort of controversy plays out in both political directions, to one degree or another. We can find a good example in Catholic social teaching, launched in its recognizable form today in Pope Leo XIII's 1891 encyclical *Rerum Novarum* (Of Revolutionary Change), which led in subsequent reflections by future popes to the concepts of *subsidiarity* and *solidarity*. On the one hand, modern left liberals wince at subsidiarity, which the *Catechism* says "is opposed to all forms of collectivism" and "sets limits for state intervention" (1885). On the other hand, modern right liberals wriggle a bit at solidarity, which, the *Catechism* explains, says that private property is fine, but that the "universal destination of goods remains primordial" (2403).

All of these issues are complicated, and this book is not the place to unravel them. Suffice it to say here that the casual observer can be forgiven for noticing what might appear to be inconsistencies, and thus be inclined to conclude that Church membership is a matter of identifying and then picking preferences.

But the more sensible take is that politics and statecraft involve a sausage-making process that inevitably drags Catholics down from the perch of the fullness of truth revealed to man in the Church. To borrow another line from the Dude from *The Big Lebowski*, "This is a very complicated case. . . . You know, a lotta ins, a lotta outs, a lotta what-have-yous." Amid navigating worldly complications, however, a Catholic may not simply think of the Faith as a religious preference into which his political priors may find an easy fit.

A Catholic Is a Catholic

There are all kinds of prefixes and adjectives that may precede the word *Catholic*. Individuals like niche identities, and the media love creating distinctions where, perhaps, none are necessary or even possible. We talk of trad Catholics, devout Catholics, fervent Catholics, conservative Catholics, orthodox Catholics, Novus Ordo Catholics, liberal Catholics, progressive Catholics, and ex-Catholics. And let us not forget the large groups of people who identify as having been raised Catholic or having gone to Catholic schools. In recent years, these last two categories have had a prodigious output of strong if not altogether informed opinions about the Church and what it means to be Catholic.

But when it comes right down to it, none of these distinctions—preferences, really—is theologically meaningful. A Catholic is a Catholic. If a person expresses a desire not to be Catholic anymore, the Church does not simply let him go. Indeed, the Church cannot. After all, if becoming Catholic were the sort of thing someone could un-become, then it would be of no value to become one in the first place. All that matters, in the end, is whether one is in a state of grace that entitles him to the fullness of communion.

But some Catholics try, in varying degrees, to express a preference for partial or total separation from their Catholic identity. In February 2024, Claire Giangravé reported in the Religion News Service that some Catholics in Italy were returning to the worship of the pagan gods of ancient Rome.[75] In November 2022, Luke Coppen reported in *The Pillar* that "debaptism" rituals were on the rise in Europe.[76] More disturbingly, in the late 1960s, the hedonistic showman Anton LaVay performed satanic parodies of weddings and baptisms.

The Catholic Church obviously wants its people to be all in, according to the formula that ancient Israel used for their relationship to God: "With all your heart, with all your soul, and with all your might" (Deut. 6:4b). Thus, when a Catholic is lacking faith, the Church describes it in at least four official ways.

First, there is *incredulity*, which the *Catechism* describes as "the neglect of revealed truth or the willful refusal to assent to it" (2089). The incredulous person is not contradicting the Church's teachings publicly and may not even have a well-developed intellectual sense of why he is having trouble believing a certain thing. Most of us, if we are honest, have been in this state, but as faith is a virtue that God's grace cultivates within us, we are not our best or truest selves when we are walking around incredulous.

Second, there is *heresy*, which the *Catechism* defines as "obstinate post-baptismal denial of some truth which must be believed" or "an obstinate doubt concerning the same." The key word here is "obstinate," which means a stubborn refusal—the sort of deliberate behavior almost all children would have gotten spanked for in days gone by. Heresy, then, is basically synonymous with preference—indeed, in the original Greek, *heresy* means "choice." But by using this word, the Church is not saying that we should be automatons. Rather, Catholicism is not presented to us an item to customize, but a package deal. Choose it, yes! But once chosen, the Catholic keeps everything that comes with it.

Third, there is *apostasy*, where a person simply declares himself not to believe what Christians believe anymore.

And finally, there is *schism*, which is the formal refusal by a Catholic or group of Catholics to submit to the pope or acknowledge communion with fellow Catholics.

In all four of these instances, the remedy is to come to the sacrament of reconciliation to confess, receive penance, and be completely forgiven. Fullness is restored, preferences are put aside, and life resumes—by no means an easy path, but the right one.

Preference Isn't All Bad

Throughout this chapter, I have attempted to show how the Catholic Church itself is no mere preference. However, within the life of a Catholic and within the life of the Catholic Church, all kinds of preferences are not only allowed, but welcome. Since to be a Catholic is to be fully human, the authentic experience of life in the world as a Catholic is full of likes and dislikes, degrees of emphasis, aesthetic variety, and the understanding that no two people's rightly ordered passions ever flow in precisely the same direction. No two Catholics have to live in the same kind of house, cheer for the same sports teams, listen to the same music, or even go to the same kind of parish church—and the reason is that the bond of unity is much deeper than any shared "preference" could express.

A Catholic is a Catholic.

Conclusion

In 1986, Peter Gabriel had a hit with the song "Big Time," in which a man with an inflated self-worth declares his liberation from the provincial values of his community of origin. He aspires to be what the American writer Tom Wolfe called a "master of the universe" in his 1987 novel *Bonfire of the Vanities*. The protagonist of Gabriel's song declares, "There's so much stuff I will own" and "I'm on my way, I'm making it." Most significantly, he imagines himself the author of his own spiritual destiny: "I will pray to a big god as I kneel in the big church," and finally, "my heaven will be a big heaven, and I will walk through the front door."

Gabriel's song, like Wolfe's novel, offers a critique by way of a caricature of the self-made man. For him, everything is always getting bigger, but is he happier or healthier than anyone else? No. And most importantly, what happens in the soul of a person who is finally his own god? "My heaven" is no heaven at all.

There is a quote, related in various ways and often falsely attributed to John Steinbeck, that says the United States does not have poor people, only temporarily embarrassed million-aires. That is, it is deeply ingrained in our psyche that there are no natural failures in the land of the free, and that only a lack of will (or someone else's cruelty) holds us back from success. Likewise, Protestantism's emphasis on an individual relationship with God and the individual Christian's interpretation of the Bible has tended to infect society, including Catholics, more widely. The result has been the problem this book addresses: a Catholic faith that we define in as many different ways as there are different individuals—a "big church," as Gabriel sings, but "big" in the wrong way.

In reality, the Faith is big in another way. This is the way that precludes any idea of "my heaven" or of using our own credentials to get in. If someone, having reached the end of this little book, should wish to reject the Catholic Church, my hope is that I have corrected the record about something this person may want no part of. I hope he is at least rejecting the real thing and not one of the boxes I have discussed in these pages.

The Faith is big, and the Church is big, because God is big. Indeed, in 1 Corinthians, which may still be the greatest document ever written about the Church, St. Paul wraps up by describing how, in the Resurrection, all things are placed in subjection under the feet of Christ the King, "that God may be everything to every one" (15:28). In this way, man feels indescribably small, with small words inadequate to express his gratitude for belonging to God. This person will inevitably face hardship and humiliation in life that make him feel smaller still, and his faith may shrink and expand throughout his life, depending on the trials he must face. Although as a Catholic he stands on the ground of everything, the sheer cliff face of nothingness strangely beckons sometimes. But at least he recognizes what is at stake. The person who belongs to Christ in the Catholic Church is not larger than life, but an integral part of a common life that is larger than him by an infinite measure. He may, in fact, look forward to taking the straight path through the narrow gate to heaven, which has already come near to him.

On the same album as "Big Time," Peter Gabriel has another song, "In Your Eyes," which portrays the point of view of almost the exact opposite sort of person. In this song, which some people wrongly interpret as merely a human love song, the man confesses at the beginning that he feels lost and empty and that he wants to run away. But something bigger and stronger keeps pulling him back from nothingness into everything. Gabriel sings, "I see the doorway to a thousand churches"—a far cry from the big man's self-styled big church. He continues, "The resolution of all the fruitless searches—I see the light and the heat. I want to be that complete."

I wonder myself whether I will ever feel truly comfortable holding the Catholic faith, just as I wonder whether I will ever fully enjoy my experience of life in the world. But in both cases, I have come to see the mark of my belonging to Christ in the Catholic Church as my inability to consider other options.

Light, heat, complete. I'm in.

The Faith. The Catholic Church.

About the Author

Andrew Petiprin is founder of and editor at the Spe Salvi Institute, a columnist at *Catholic World Report*, and host of the Ignatius Press Podcast. He is co-author of *Popcorn with the Pope: A Guide to the Vatican Film List* and author of *Truth Matters: Knowing God and Yourself.* Andrew was a British Marshall Scholar at Oxford University, and he also holds degrees from Yale University and the University of Pittsburgh. He is the former Fellow of Popular Culture at the Word on Fire Institute, and he has written for various publications, including *The Catholic Herald*, *The Lamp*, *The European Conservative*, *The American Conservative*, and *Evangelization & Culture*. A former Episcopal priest, Andrew came into full communion with the Catholic Church in 2019. He and his family live in north Texas.

Endnotes

1. "First Apology of Justin, the Martyr," ed. and trans. Edward Rochie Hardy, in *Early Christian Fathers* (New York: Touchstone, 1996), 245.

2. "Octavius," ch. 30, eds. Alexander Roberts, James Donaldson, and A. Cleveland Coxe, from *Ante-Nicene Fathers*, vol. 4 (Buffalo, NY: Christian Literature Publishing Company, 1885), trans. Robert Ernest Wallis. Available online at https://www.newadvent.org/fathers/0410.htm, ed. Kevin Knight.

3. John Henry Newman, *Apologia Pro Vita Sua* (New York: Norton, 1968), 97.

4. C.S. Lewis, *Mere Christianity* (New York: HarperOne, 2001), XV.

5. C.S. Lewis, *The Silver Chair* (New York: HarperTrophy, 2000), 21.

6. Russell Kirk, *The Conservative Mind: From Burke to Eliot* (Washington, D.C.: Gateway Editions, 1985), 7-8.

7. Karl Marx and Friedrich Engels, *The Communist Manifesto* in *Economic and Philosophic Manuscripts of 1844 and the Communist Manifesto* (Amherst, NY: Prometheus Books, 1988), 208.

8. Luigi Giussani, *Why the Church?*, trans. Viviane Hewitt (Montreal: McGill-Queen's University Press, 2001), 54.

9. Kate Ng, "What is the history of the word 'woke' and its modern uses?" *The Independent*, January 22, 2021. Available online at https://www.independent.co.uk/news/uk/home-news/woke-meaning-word-history-b1790787.html.

10. Matthew Petrusek, *Evangelization and Ideology: How to Understand and Respond to the Political Culture* (Park Ridge, Il: Word on Fire Institute, 2023), 301.

11. C.S. Lewis, *The Last Battle* (New York: HarperCollins, 2000), 161.

12. See https://chat.openai.com/share/e258ccbb-3931-41a5-ac97-d752a67a9f3f.

13. Pew Research Center, "Religious Landscape Study," available online at www.pewresearch.org/religion/religious-landscape-study.

14. Emo Philips, "The best God joke ever—and it's mine!" *The Guardian*, September 29, 2005. Available online at https://www.theguardian.com/stage/2005/sep/29/comedy.religion.

15. "Baptism, Eucharist, and Ministry," Faith and Order Paper No. 111 (Geneva: World Council of Churches, 1982), 5. Available online at https://www.oikoumene.org/sites/default/files/Document/FO1982_111_en.pdf.

16. "An Agreed Statement on the Lima Document: 'Baptism, Eucharist, and Ministry,'" United States Conference of Catholic Bishops, October 27, 1984. Available online at https://www.usccb.org/committees/ecumenical-interreligious-affairs/agreed-statement-lima-document-baptism-eucharist-and.

17. "America's Wars," Department of Veterans Affairs, Office of Public Affairs, November 2023. Available online at www.va.gov/opa/publications/factsheets/fs_americas_wars.pdf.

18. "Background: American Catholics and World War I," in "American Catholic Women's Participation in Twentieth

Century World Wars," American Catholic History Classroom at The Catholic University of America, updated September 16, 2024. Available online at https://guides.lib.cua.edu/c.php?g=1410360&p=10444235.

19. "Background: American Catholics and World War II" in "American Catholic Women's Participation in Twentieth Century World Wars," American Catholic history Classroom at the Catholic University of America, updated September 16, 2024. Available online at https://guides.lib.cua.edu/c.php?g=1410360&p=10444712.

20. Fulton Sheen, *Life Is Worth Living: First and Second Series* (San Francisco: Ignatius, 1999), 107.

21. Henri de Lubac, *Catholicism: Christ and the Common Destiny of Man* (San Francisco: Ignatius, 1988), 25.

22. *Apologia Pro Vita Sua*, 96.

23. *Euthyphro*, trans. G.M.A. Grube in *Plato: Complete Works*, ed. John M. Cooper (Indianapolis: Hackett, 1997), 23-24b.

24. Ibid., 6a.

25. *Phaedo* in *Complete Works*, 100.

26. Ibid., 63e.

27. "First Apology of Justin," ed. and trans. Edward Rochie Hardy in *Early Christian Fathers*, ed. Cyril C. Richardson (New York: Touchstone, 1996), 272.

28. *City of God*, trans. William Babcock (Hyde Park, NY: New City Press, 2012), 54.

29. Ibid., VI.2.

30. Ibid., I.31.

31. Ibid., II.29.

32. Ibid., VIII.27.

33. Ibid., VII.19.25.

34. *Confessions*, trans. R.S. Pine-Coffin (New York: Penguin Classics, 1961), VII.14.

35. "Homily of His Eminence Card. Joseph Ratzinger, Dean of the College of Cardinals," Vatican Basilica, April 18, 2005. Available online at http://www.vatican.va/gpII/documents /homily-pro-eligendo-pontifice_20050418_en.html.

36. Pope Benedict XVI, "Monotheism and Tolerance" in *What is Christianity? The Last Writings* (San Francisco: Ignatius, 2023), 46.

37. "Why America's 'nones' don't identify with a religion," Pew Research Center, August 8, 2018. Available online at https://www.pewresearch.org/short-reads/2018/08/08/why -americas-nones-dont-identify-with-a-religion.

38. Kate Julian, "Why are young people having so little sex?" *The Atlantic*, December 2018. Available online at https://www.theatlantic .com/magazine/archive/2018/12/the-sex-recession/573949.

39. *Confessions*, VIII.17.

40. "The Holy Father's General Audience Address of December 6, 2000," *L'Osservatore Romano*. Vatican, December 13, 2000. Available online at https://www.catholicculture.org/culture /library/view.cfm?recnum=3274.

41. Tyler Arnold, "Today the Church honors three groups of martyrs as Christians worldwide continue to face persecution," *Catholic News Agency*, January 12, 2024. Available online at https://www.catholicnewsagency.com/news/256521/today-the -church-honors-3-groups-of-martyrs-as-christians-worldwide -continue-to-face-persecution.

42. R. Cavanagh, "Catholicism in Nigeria: The Church stays strong while facing terrorism, persecution," *Catholic World Report*, October 7, 2020. Available online at https://www

.catholicworldreport.com/2020/10/07/catholicism-in-nigeria -the-church-stays-strong-while-facing-terrorism-persecution.

43. "The Church in Africa, by the numbers," *The Pillar*, February 3, 2023. Available online at https://www.pillarcatholic.com/p /the-church-in-africa-by-the-numbers.

44. T.S. Eliot, "The Idea of a Christian Society" in *Christianity and Culture* (New York: Harvest, 1968), 34.

45. "Public Trust in Government: 1958-2024," Pew Research Center, June 24, 2024. Available online at https://www.pewresearch.org /politics/2023/09/19/public-trust-in-government-1958-2023.

46. Cormac McCarthy, *The Road* (New York: Vintage, 2006), 278-279.

47. Ibid., 273.

48. "Email From Erika Christakis: 'Dressing Yourselves,' email to Silliman College (Yale) Students on Halloween Costumes," FIRE (Foundation for Individual Rights and Expression). Available online at https://www.thefire.org/email from erika -christakis-dressing-yourselves-email-to-silliman-college-yale -students-on-halloween-costumes.

49. Greg Lukianoff and Jonathan Haidt, "The Coddling of the American Mind," *The Atlantic*, September 2015. Available online at https://www.theatlantic.com/magazine/archive/2015/09 /the-coddling-of-the-american-mind/399356.

50. Kevin Fagan, "SF homeless population swells by 17% in latest tally," *San Francisco Chronicle*, May 17, 2019. Available online at https://www.sfchronicle.com/bayarea/article/SF-homeless -population-swells-by-17-in-latest-13851897.php?psid=hBcsm.

51. Sam Levin, "Los Angeles homeless population hits 36,000 in dramatic rise," *The Guardian*, June 4, 2019. Available online at https://www. theguardian.com/us-news/2019/jun/04/los-angeles-homeless -population-city-county. See also "2019 Greater Los Angeles

Homeless Count Presentation," updated June 17, 2020. Available on-line at https://www.lahsa.org/documents?id=3437-2019-greater-los-angeles-homeless-count-presentation.pdf.

52. *The Poetry of Robert Frost*, ed. Edward Connery Lathem (New York: Holt, Rinehart and Winston, 1969), 38.

53. *The Complete Works of Aristotle, Volume Two*, trans. Ingram Bywater, ed. Jonathan Barnes (Princeton: Princeton University Press, 1995), 2,324.

54. *Apologia pro Vita Sua*, 156.

55. John Henry Newman, *Loss and Gain* (San Francisco: Ignatius, 2012), 176.

56. "Battle of Gettysburg," *The World Book Encyclopedia: Volume 8* (Chicago: World Book Inc.), 176.

57. Ibid., "Battle of the Bulge," *Volume 1*, 694.

58. "Research Starters: Worldwide Deaths in World War II," The National World War Two Museum, New Orleans. Available online at https://www.nationalww2museum.org/students-teachers/student-resources/research-starters/research-starters-worldwide-deaths-world-war.

59. Pascal, *Pensées* (*Great Books of the Western World*, vol. 33), trans. W.F. Trotter (Chicago: Encyclopedia Britannica, 1952), 205.

60. Another of the "Moral Tales," *La Collectioneuse*, was actually the third film released in the series in 1967. Rohmer insisted that *Maud* be numbered third in the series as intended, because he could not shoot it when he wanted to.

61. Antoine de Baecque and Noël Herpe, *Éric Rohmer: A Biography*, trans. Steven Rendall and Lisa Neal (New York: Columbia University Press, 2016), 230-231.

62. Vittorio Hösle, *Éric Rohmer: Filmmaker and Philosopher* (New York: Bloomsbury, 2016), 20.

63. *Éric Rohmer: A Biography*, 228.

64. "Blaise Pascal" in *The Encyclopedia of Religion*, vol. 11 (New York: Macmillan, 1987), 203.

65. This section is adapted from my article "Rohmer on Joy," in *Evangelization & Culture*, issue no. 14, Winter 2022. Reproduced with permission of the editor.

66. John Henry Newman, "A Letter Addressed to the Duke of Norfolk on Occasion of Mr. Gladstone's Recent Expostulation, Certain Difficulties Felt by Anglicans in Catholic Teaching, Volume 2," ch. 3, sec. 2. Available online at https://www.newmanreader.org/works/anglicans/volume2/gladstone/section3.html.

67. Ibid., ch. 3, sec. 5.

68. Pascal, *Pensées*, trans. A.J. Krailsheimer (New York: Penguin, 1995), 122.

69. Daniel and Bethany Meola, *Life-Giving Wounds: A Catholic Guide to Healing for Adult Children of Divorce or Separation* (San Francisco: Ignatius, 2023), 165.

70. Henri de Lubac, *Catholicism: Christ and the Common Destiny of Man*, trans. Lancelot C. Sheppard and Sr. Elizabeth Englund, OCD (San Francisco: Ignatius, 1988), 76.

71. James T. McHugh, "Catholics and the 1996 Election," *First Things*, February 1997. Available online at https://www.firstthings.com/article/1997/02/002-catholics-and-the-election.

72. Kevin Christopher Robles, "Voting Catholic: How have Catholics voted in past elections?" *America Magazine*, October 3, 2020. Available online at https://www.americamagazine.org/politics-society/2020/10/03/voting-catholic-how-have-catholics-voted-past-elections.

73. Frank Newport, "Religious Group Voting and the 2020 Election," *Gallup*, November 13, 2020. Available online at

https://news.gallup.com/opinion/polling-matters/324410/
religious-group-voting-2020-election.aspx.

74. Salvatore J. Cordileone, "Letter to the faithful on the Notifica-
tion sent to Speaker Nancy Pelosi," Archdiocese of San Francisco, May 20, 2022. Available online at https://sfarchdiocese
.org/letter-to-the-faithful-on-the-notification-sent-to-speaker
-nancy-pelosi.

75. Claire Giangravé, "Ex-Catholics in Rome reconnect with roots,
spirituality in paganism," *Religious News Service*, February 21, 2024.
Available online at https://religionnews.com/2024/02/21/ex
-catholics-in-rome-reconnect-with-roots-spirituality-in-pa-
ganism.

76. Luke Coppen, "Belgium sees sharp rise in 'debaptism' requests," *The Pillar*, December 1, 2022. Available online at
https://www.pillarcatholic.com/p/belgium-sees-sharp-rise-in
-debaptism-requests.